# SOUTHAMPTON INSTITUTE

introduction////graphic/interpretation/of/the/swiss/designer////environment////codes////habits
name/design/company////happypets

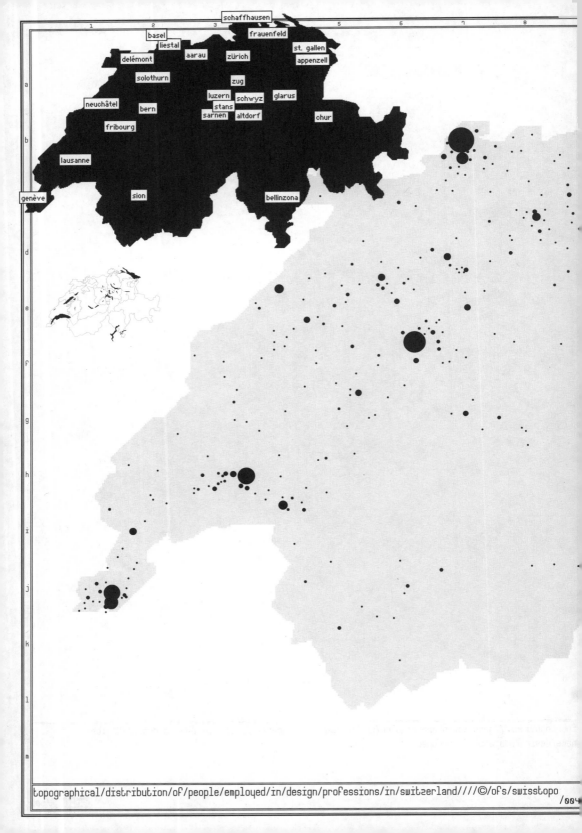

schaffhausen

basel
liestal
delémont    aarau    zürich    frauenfeld
solothurn            zug    st. gallen
                                appenzell
neuchâtel    bern    luzern    schwyz    glarus
                     stans
fribourg             sarnen    altdorf         chur

lausanne

genève

sion                          bellinzona

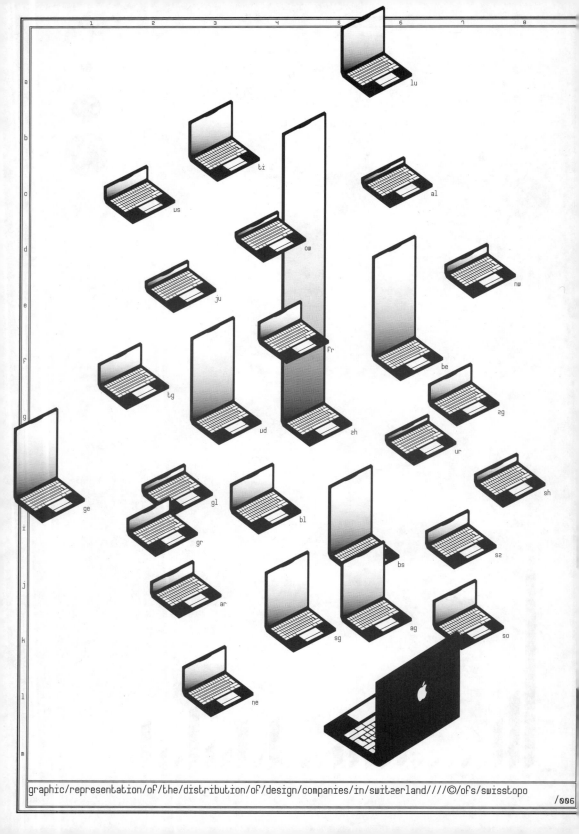

500
400
300
200
100
000

zh be lu ur sz ow nw gl zg fr so bs bl sh ar al sg gr ag tg ti ud us ne ge ju fl

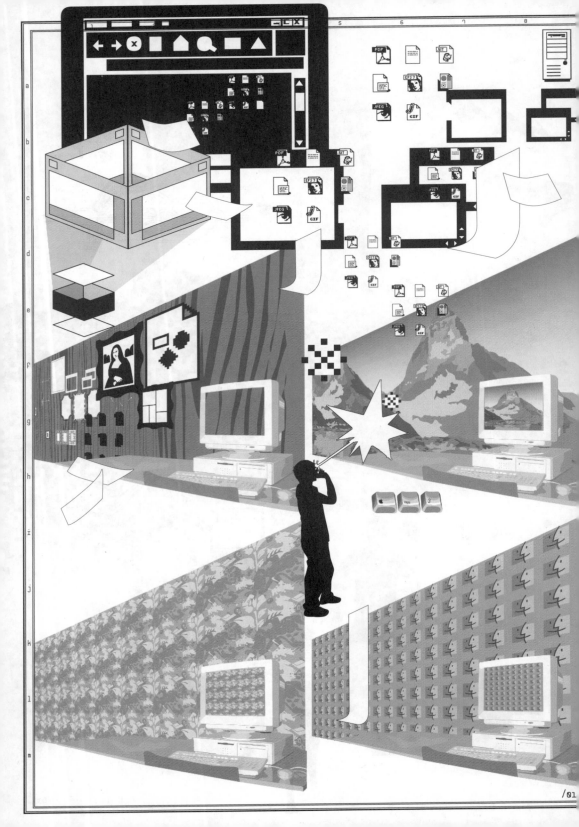

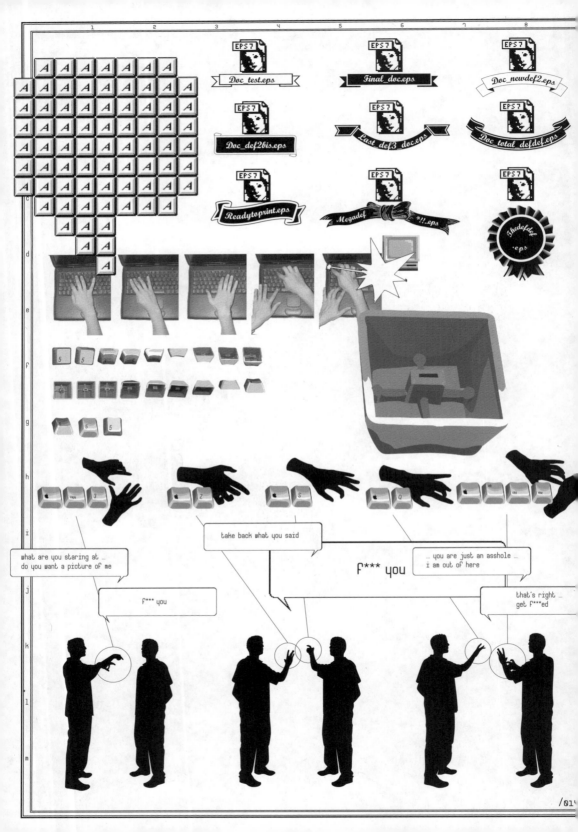

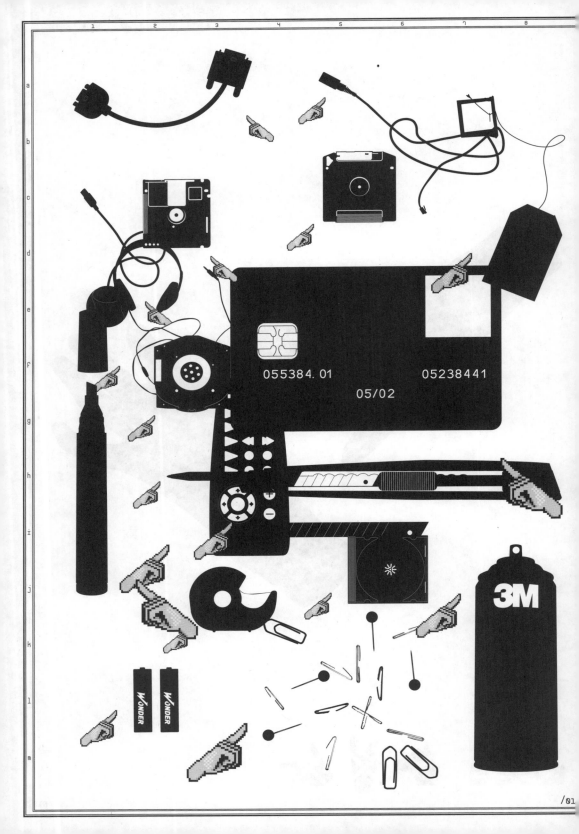

055384. 01          05238441

05/02

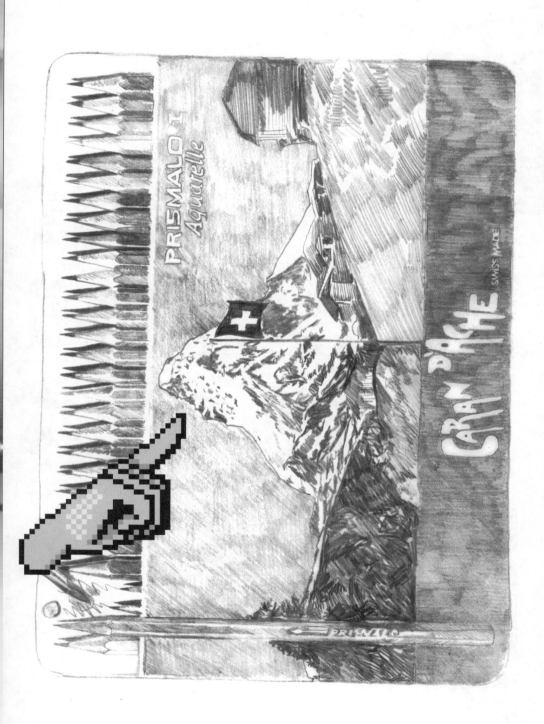

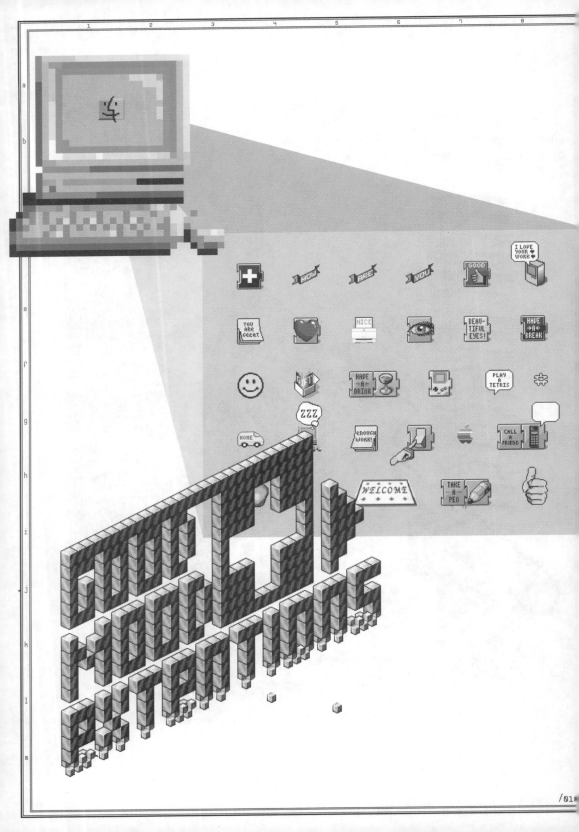

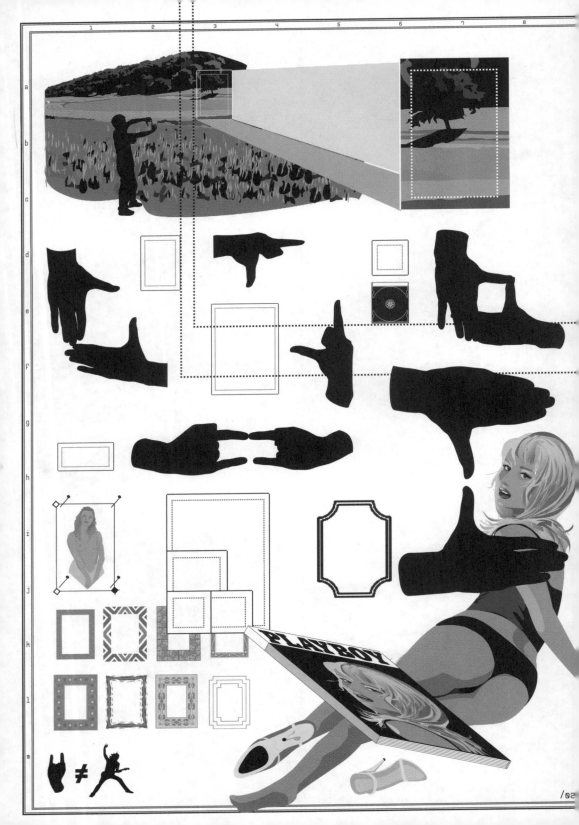

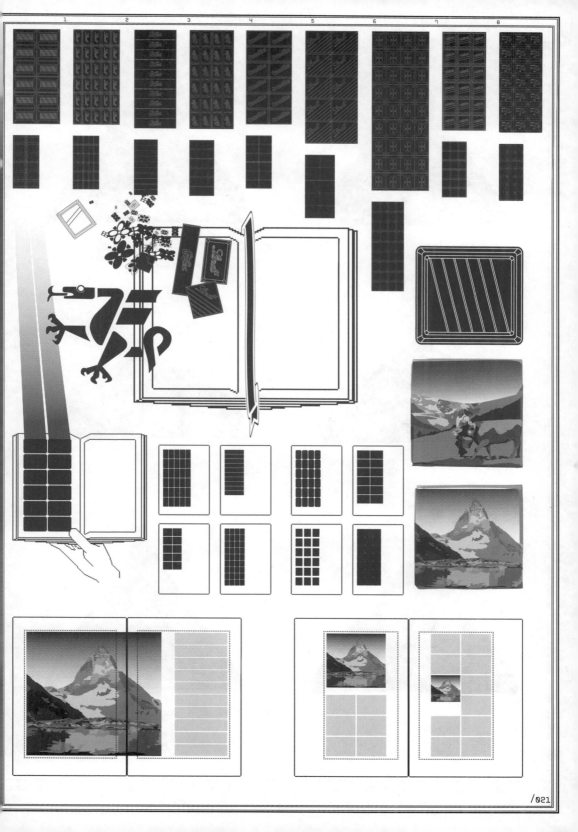

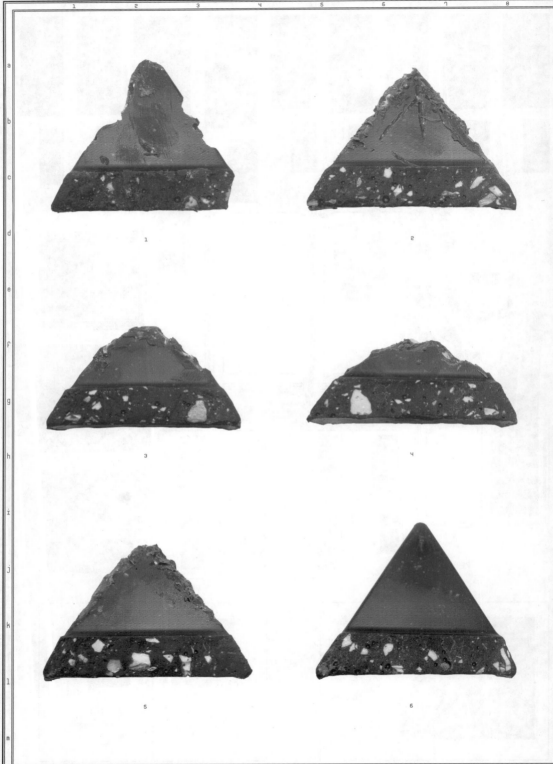

1 ////matterhorn//// 2 ////dent/blanche//// 3 ////eiger//// 4 ////jungfrau//// 5 ////weisshorn//// 6 ////toblerhorn

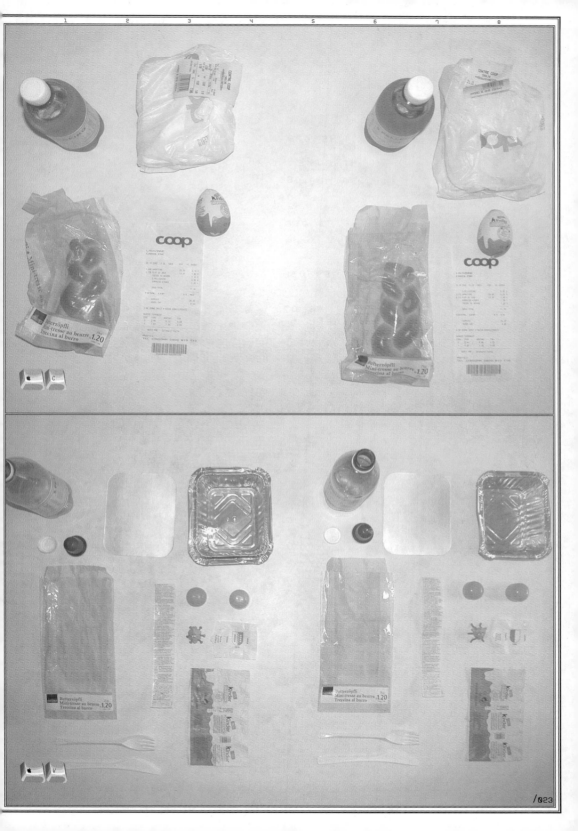

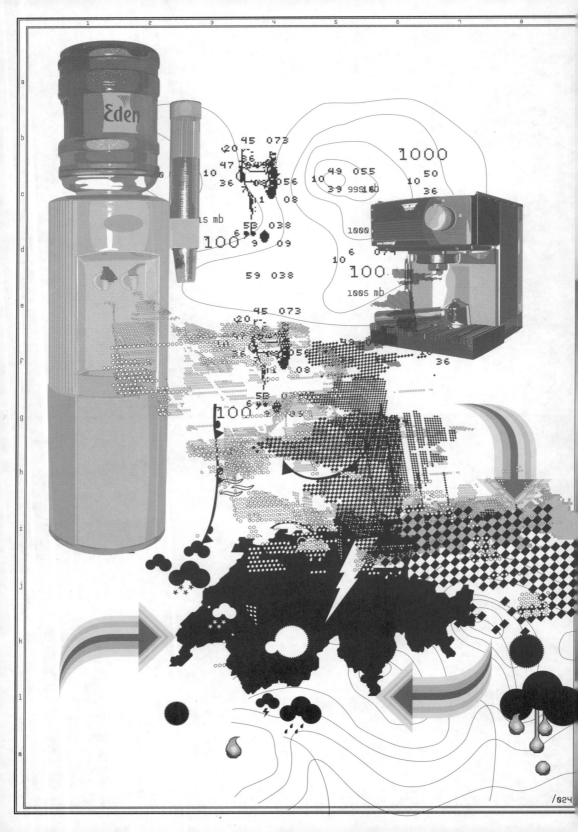

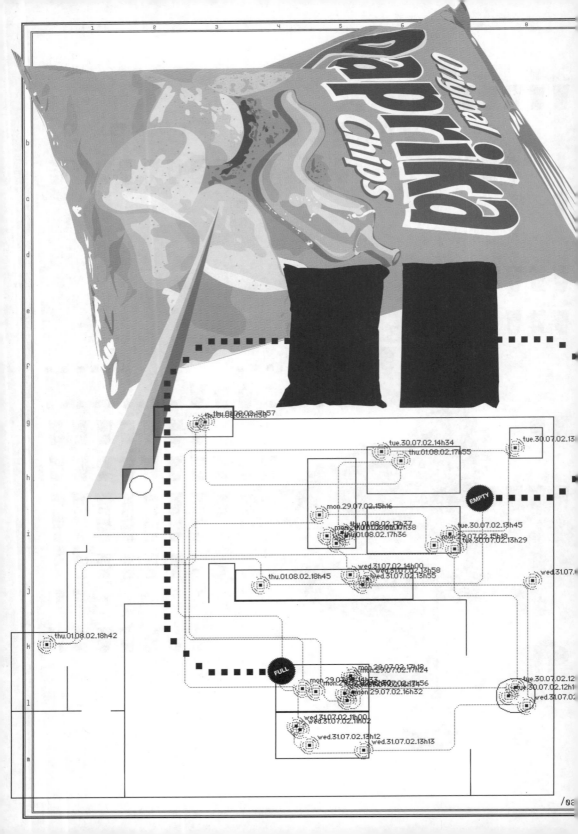

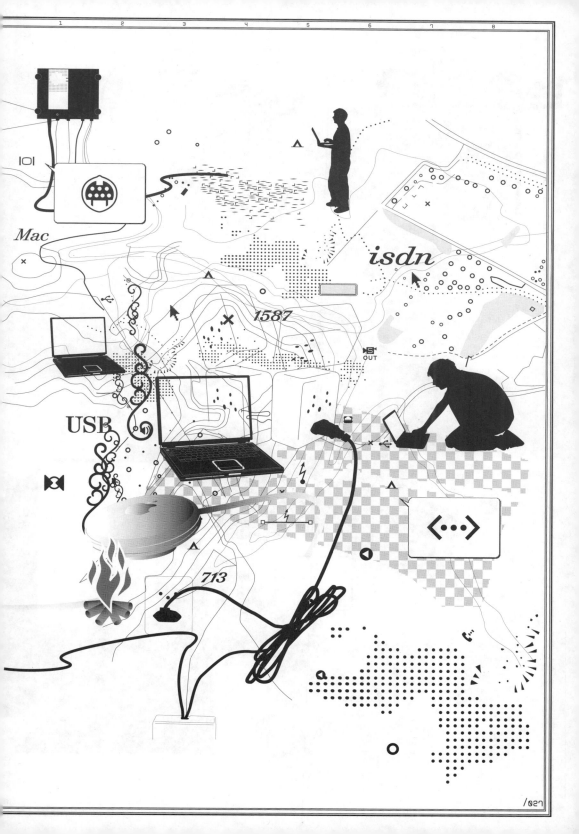

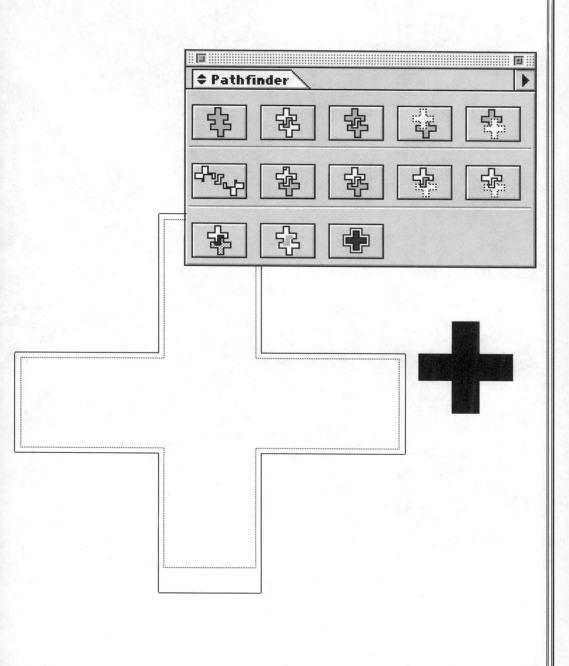

works////selection/of/graphix/created/by/swiss/designers
name/design/company//// //diy////a---b////aubry/bastien////born/julia////cottenceau/geoffrey////
electronic/curry/ltd////fulguro.////gtu////güdel/benjamin////happypets////kappeler/marc////brunner/bianca/
//moiré////la3l////lehmann/aude////mentary.com////norm////paulus/lauris////raar////sonderegger/alex////
woodtli/martin

Nicolas Pages

*Septembre*

Flammarion

Flash

Trop tard

Jardin d'hiver

Score: 15

You made a correct guess!

G     is
THE BES

_ETTER

Your guess: □   Trouve la phrase   R _ C K

*BCD*FGH*JKLMN*PQ*S*UVWXYZ

Higher

Be local   cadavres

exquis

TRUST
no one
just DO IT
YOURSELF

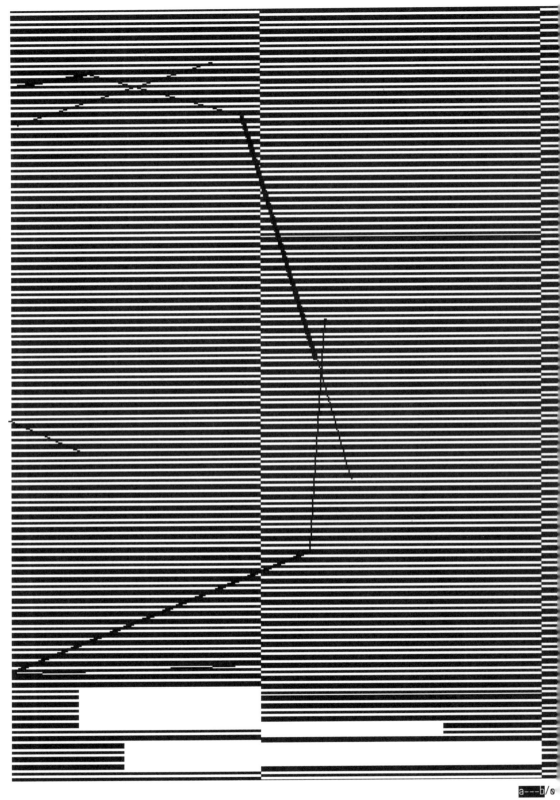

a---b/o

ABCDEFGHIJ
KLMNOPQRS
TUVWXYZO
123456789

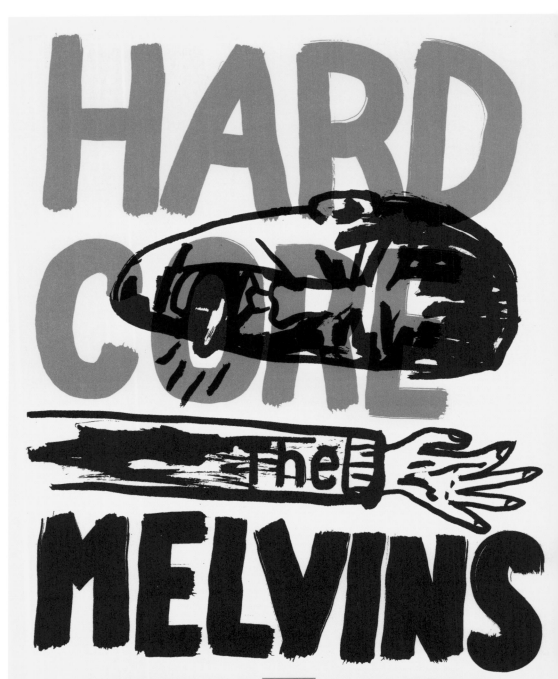

# HARD
# CORE
# the
# MELVINS

## ROTE FABRIK: SO.11.MÄRZ
### Aktionshalle, 21.00 Uhr

Vorverkauf benützen! **Zürich:** BIZZ, Jamarico, Jelmoli City, Migros City, Crazy Beat, Rec Rec,
**St. Gallen:** Bro Records, **Winterthur:** Musicbox, **Baden:** Zero Zero, **Aarau:** Dezibelle, **Luzern:** Doo Bop, **Bern:** Chop Records.

aubry/bastien/0

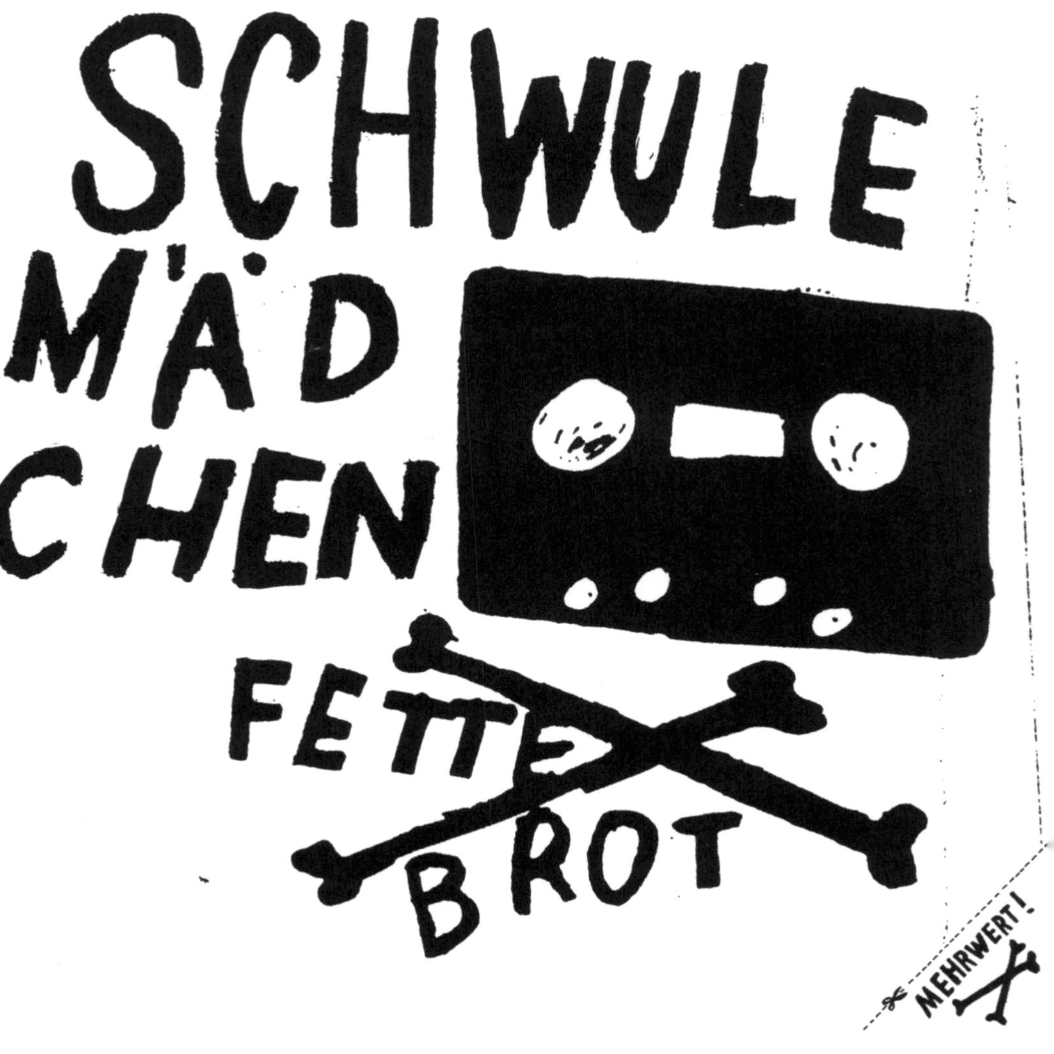
SCHWULE
MÄD
CHEN
FETTE
BROT
MEHRWERT!

(Calvino)

...ng VEDUTE.

...n reserveren niet mogelijk

...r meer informatie

stichting VEDUTE. - vrijdag 14 - 17h

Tussen de Bogen 42 - 1013 JB Amsterdam - T (020 827.6346)

met dank aan

Stimuleringsfonds voor Architectuur

Amsterdams Fonds voor de Kunst

ontwerp DJ

zeefdruk Kees Maas

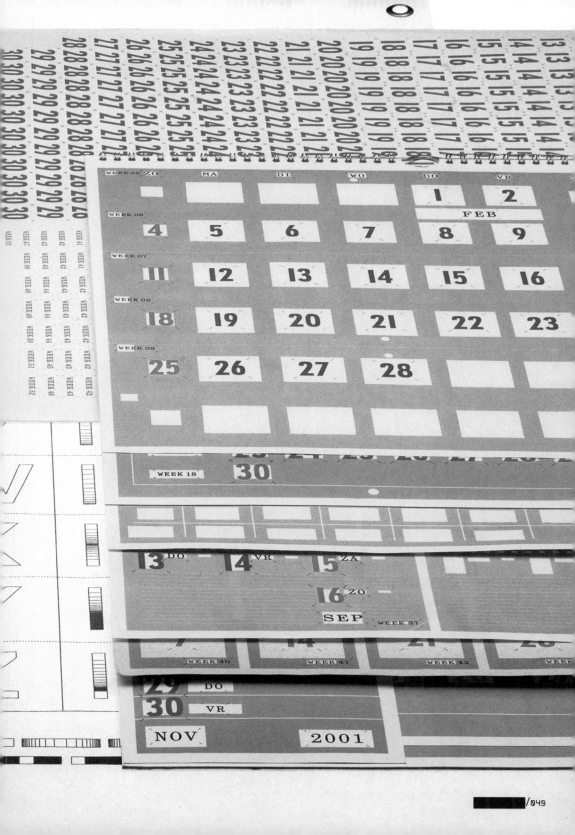

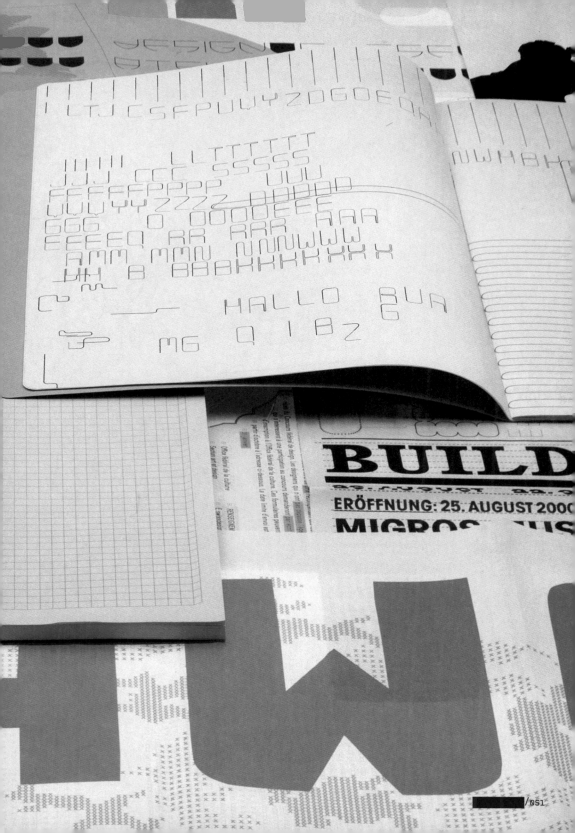

PLACE PHOTO HERE

# PLACE PHOTO HERE

NEW YORK CITY©

IN GOD SOME TRUST – IN CAR ALL RUST

LA VÉRITÉE:
LA VÉRITÉE EST
PLUS GRANDE
QUE 12 MOUTONS
ET
DE TRÈS HAUT
LES TRÈS
HAUTS TOMBENT
AUSSI

# INNATANDA
# LA VÉRITÉ REVÉ-
# LÉE

NO GOUVERNEMENT

JUST GO HOME
JUST GO HOME
JUST GO HOME
JUST GO HOME

JUST GO HOME
JUST GO HOME
JUST GO HOME

JUST GO HOM
JUST GO HOM
JUST GO HOM
JUST GO HOM

"MEN WOULD RATHER HAVE THEIR FILL OF SLEEP, LOVE, AND SINGING AND DANCING THAN OF WAR," SAID HOMER. THE EDITORS OF AVANT-GARDE AGREE, AND DO HEREBY ISSUE A CALL FOR ENTRIES FOR AN INTERNATIONAL POSTER COMPETITION BASED ON THIS THEME:

# NO MORE WAR!

Judges: Richard Avedon, Leonard Baskin, Alexander Calder, Milton Glaser, Art Kane, Jack Levine, Herb Lubalin, Dwight Macdonald, Robert Motherwell, Robert Osborn, Larry Rivers, Ben Shahn, Edward Steichen & Sloan Wilson.

AVANT GARDE

I WANT YOU TO SING

# NO MORE PIPE-
# LINES 2001™

STOP BAD BREATHS NOW

# PEOPLE MEAN
# PEACE™

PEACE AND RESPECT LOVE

SEE

vendredi 23 juin 2m, dès 21h33
bistrok', 24 boulevard des philosophes, genève

samedi 24 juin 2m, dès 21h33
nernier, festival de la zikmu, la france

SEX

vendredi 23 juin 2m, dès 21h33
bistrok', 24 boulevard des philosophes, genève

samedi 24 juin 2m, dès 21h33
nernier, festival de la zikmu, la france

SUN

vendredi 23 juin 2m, dès 21h33
bistrok', 24 boulevard des philosophes, genève

samedi 24 juin 2m, dès 21h33
nernier, festival de la zikmu, la france

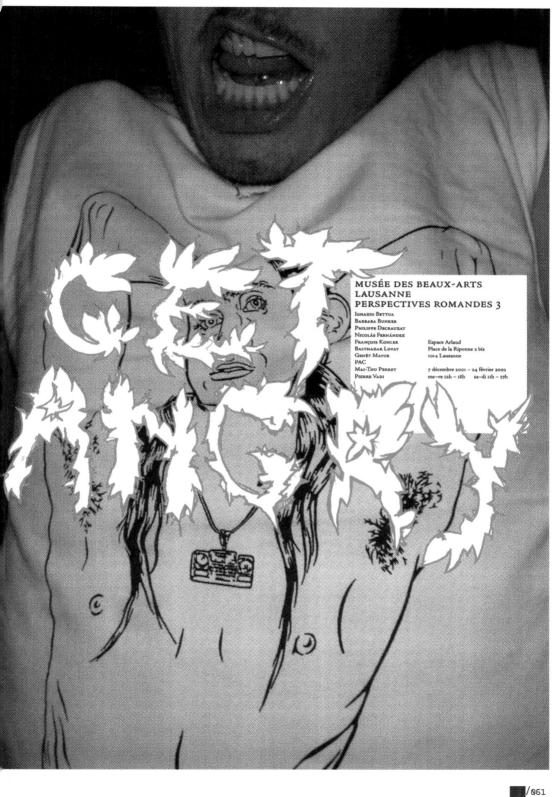

MUSÉE DES BEAUX-ARTS
LAUSANNE
PERSPECTIVES ROMANDES 3

Ignazio Bettua
Barbara Bunker
Philippe Decrauzat
Nicolás Fernández
François Kohler          Espace Arlaud
Balthazar Lovay         Place de la Riponne 2 bis
Genêt Mayor            1014 Lausanne
PAC
Mai-Thu Perret         7 décembre 2001 – 24 février 2002
Pierre Vadi            me–ve 12h – 18h    sa–di 11h – 17h

UNIVERSITÉ POPULAIRE
DE LAUSANNE

best regards,

gtv

gudel/benjamin/o

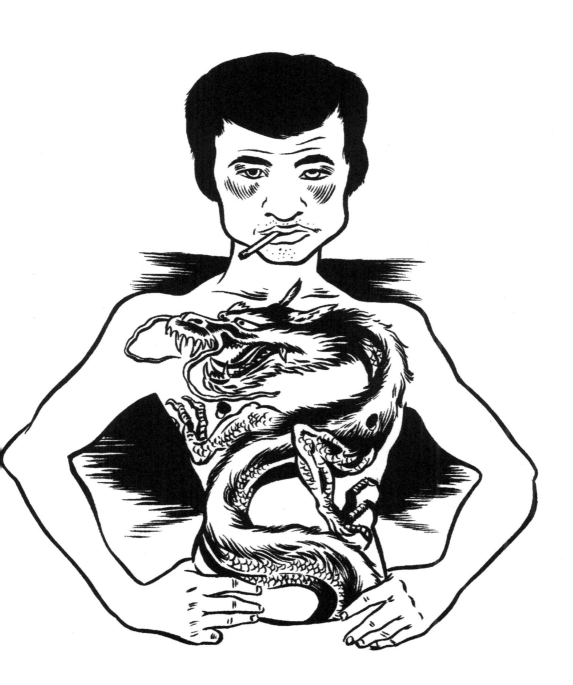

IRON MAIDEN

new print...
new polenisation.

kino

14/15/08

20. wuhr
platzfest
langenthal

16
bis
19/08

Do/14/08/Dancer
in The Dark

Mi/15/08/Buena
Vista Socia' Club

Jewells ab 18:00 Küche
und Bar
Filmbeginn: 21:00

patronat stadt

amt für kultur
kanton bern

Do/15/08/ab18:30
/Einladung
zum Apéritif
/Gala-Abend
mit Kulinaritäten/mit Ueli
Dichsel, Werner Bodinek,
Clo Bisaz, Single Cells u.v.a.

Fr/17/08/19:30 Büne
Huber/22:00 Gustav /00:0˚
futurelounge

Sa/18/08/09:00 Markt/ab 13:30 Figuren-
theater/19:00 Longhi+Larghi's Fahrräté (UK)
/20:00 The Tarantinos (UK)
/22:00 Sneaker
pimps (UK)
/00.00 Future-
lounge. Ganzer Tag Bar
und Essen

So/19/08
/10:00 bis 13:00
Brunch
auf dem
Wuhrplatz

mehr infos s. programmheft

www.wuhrplatzfest.ch

kino

01/16/00/Dancer
In The Dark

Mi/15/08/Buena
Vista Social Club

Jewells ab 18:00 Kuche
und Bar
Filmbeginn: 21:00

enthal

amt für kultur
kanton bern

Do/16/08/ab18:30
/Einladung
zum Apéritiv
/Gala-Abend
mit Kulinaritaten/mit Ueli
Bichsel, Werner Godinek,
Clo Bisaz, Single Cells u.v.a.

Fr/17/08/19:30 Büne
Huber/22:ω Gustav /00:00
futurelounge

Sa/18/08/09-00 Markt/ab 13:3 Figuren-
theater/19:00 Longhi•Larghi's Fahrgäté
/20:00 The Tarantinos[UK]
/22:00 Sneaker
pimps[UK]
/00.00 Future-
lounge. Ganzer Tag Bar
und Essen

So/19/08
/10:00 bis 13:00
Brunch
auf dem
Wartgarte

hr in

nmheft

ww wuhprausi st.ch

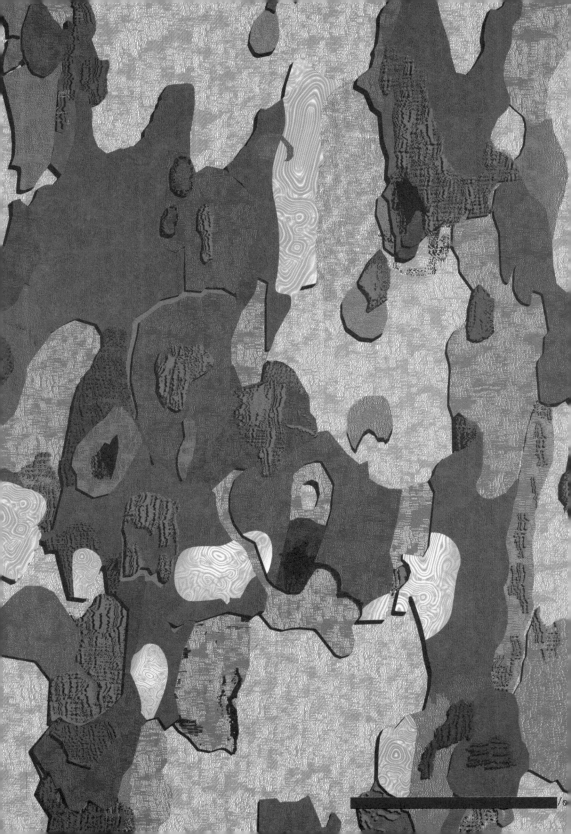

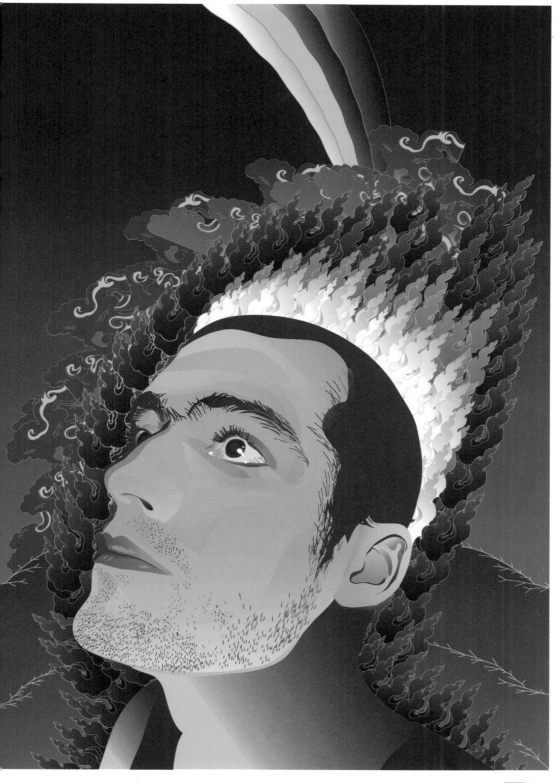

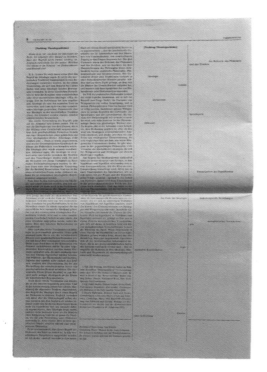

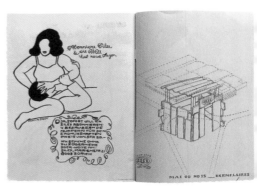

Albisetti, Lehmann, Shahbazi

1–6
Lithos, Druck: Ateliers Jeune, Bern
180 kr. Zürich, 2001.

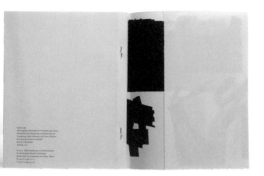

PAST IS GONE...
AND FUTURE IS
SO EXPENSIVE.

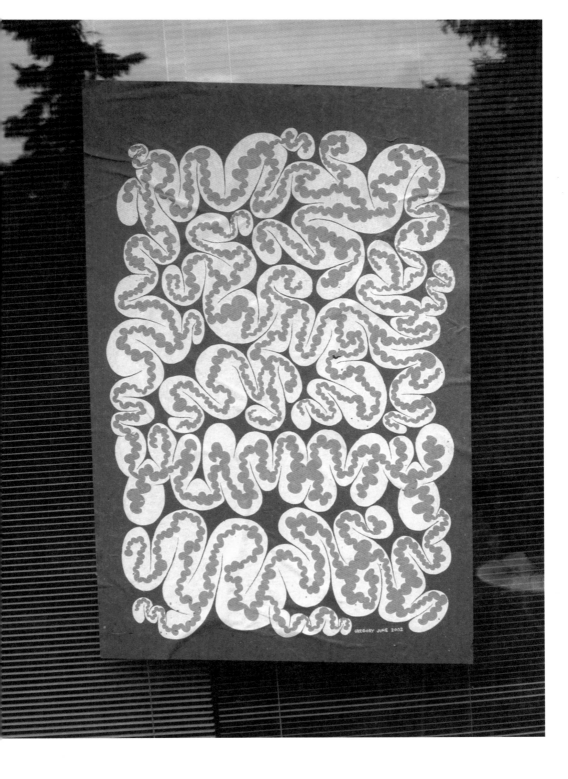

▽ 🗁 DKS
 ▽ 🗁 NORM DOKS
  ▽ 🗁 INTRODUCTION
   ▷ 🗋 INTRODUCTION.DEF 01.01.2000

norm/⊙

# LABORPROBEN ■■■■■■T−

Bei... wenn nicht gegenteilige Ansichten stossen wir allerdings,

...beruhen vornehmlich

...Zeichen; es verpflichtet den

...Anschauungsgrundlage

...festmachen lassen.

So und anders.

▽ 📁 DKS
  ▽ 📁 JOB DOKS
    ▷ 📁 HGKZ
      ▷ 📄 HGKZ.DEF 01.06.2000

# 0:
# TROTZDEM/DESHALB
# 1:
# BIG SNEAKER (
# THE NINETIES              )
# 2:
# A SHORT CATALOGUE
# OF THINGS THAT YOU THINK YOU WANT

> SO, WHAT IS IT THAT YOU THINK YOU WANT? THE RECEIVED WISDOM GOES THAT YOU WANT FAME, THAT WE ALL WANT IT NOW, THE SAME WAY OUR PARENTS WANTED A GOOD MELON. BUT IT ONLY MEANS ONE THING, IT HAS ONLY EVER MEANT ONE THING: MORE PEOPLE KNOWING YOU THAN YOU KNOW PEOPLE. EVERYTHING ELSE IS A ... ACCESSORY. MONEY, GOOD CLOTHES, CARS – YOU CAN GET THESE ELSEWHERE, JUST DON'T BOTHER WITH THIS THING, MORE PEOPLE KNOWING YOU THAN YOU KNOW PEOPLE. SHUN IT. PUT A BLACK CROSS OVER YOUR DOOR. IT'S NO CURE, IT'S JUST FOR PEOPLE WHO HAVE LOST SOMETHING. AMPUTEES. WHAT ELSE? WELL, YOU WANT MUSCLE DEFINITION AND AT ANY COST. NOTHING I CAN SAY CAN CONVINCE YOU OTHERWISE, AND YOU WILL GET YOUR TRAINER AND YOUR HOME GYM, EVEN THOUGH I AM NOT ALONE AND THERE ARE OTHERS WHO WOULD LIKE TO TOUCH YOU, SOFT AS YOU ARE, IN THIS HARD CITY . BUT YOU THINK HARDNESS IS WHAT YOU NEED TO SURVIVE THESE DAYS, AND MAYBE YOU ARE RIGHT. I CAN'T FIGHT YOU (I'D LOSE). HOW WOULD ANYONE TELLS ME YO U WANT SOMETHING THAT'S COMFY LIKE A SOFA BUT DOESN'T LOOK LIKE A SOFA, BECAUSE YOU HATE THE SUBURBS AND YOU NEVER WANT TO GO BACK THERE. BUT AT THE SAME TIME YOU APPRECIATE THE FACT THAT EVERYBODY'S GOT TO SIT DOWN. THING IS A LOVABLE SENTIMENT. ONLY, IT WASN'T THE SOFA THAT MADE LIFE SUBURBAN, AND IT WASN'T THE CURTAINS OR THE CARPET OR THE DEADLY TRIM. NO MATTER HOW CHEAPER THAN THE HARD NO AMOUNT OF WOOD FLOWERS AND CORIAN FURNITURE AND JAPANESE WALL PRINTS WILL CHANGE WHAT'S IN THE MARROW OF YOU AND WANT IT ... . OF SOMEONE BETTER LOOKING THAN US. MAYBE YOU HAVE SOMEONE BETTER LOOKING THAN YOU SITTING RIGHT NEXT TO YOU N..OW, READING OVER YOUR SHOULDER. STROKING THE NAPE OF YOUR NE..CK. IT'S LIKE HAVING THE TV ON, ISN'T IT? SHINY, PRETTY, DISTRACTING. YOU'VE GOT HUMAN TV ALL THE TIME , YOU LUCKY THING. YOU REALLY DON'T NEED ... THAT YOU WANT A BIG SHINY CAUSE YOU CAN GET BEHIND AND, FRIENDS, I CAN SEE YOUR P..OINT. AFTER ALL, YOUR GREAT-GRANDFATHER ... OUR GRANDFATHER ... THEN Y OUR D..AD GOT THE SIXTIES. WHAT DID YOU GET? BUPKISS. OR RATHER, A WHOLE LOAD OF INTRICATE CLAIMS AND COUNTER-CLAIMS, CIVIL CONFLICTS INVOLVING FIVE DIFFERENT FACTIONS, FIGHTS T.HAT LOOK LIKE WRONGS AND VICE VERSA. FEELS LIKE TOO MUCH SOMETIMES, HUH? YOU'D LIKE THINGS A LITTLE SIMPLER, MORE BLACK AND WHITE. WELL, YOU'R ... L OVER. FRANKLY, EVERYONE'S TIRED ... PROTECTING YOU FROM WHAT SOME PEOPLE DEAL WITH EVERY DAY. BEST ADVICE I CAN GIVE YOU IS START SMALL. SORT OUT YOUR BATHROOM CABINET AND GO FROM THERE WISH ... EXPRESS SO. ANYTIME ANYTHING, WELL W..ANT IT, BUT KNOW WHAT IT SURELY ANY RIGHT-MINDED 21ST -CENTURY TYPE WANTS TO ... GET US ... OVER, WHEREVER ... T ... A GECAF CHOICE ... RE, IF YOU LET THEM, IN ... E PLAY ... TRAINERS WITH ... S THE GLOBE. NO, I COULDN'T IT'S YOU'RE WANTING. I READ THAT LEONARDO CALL ... .... ... .... URE WHICH TAKES THE NEEDS OF A FAT WHITE AMERICAN AND REPRODUCES THEM ... WORLDS S THE GLOBE. NO, I COULDN'T BELIEVE HE SAID ANYTHING THAT SMART. EITHER, SPEAKING WHICH ... I YOU STILL WISH ... ... ... BE WITH THE PERFECT A ... CA. UTOPIARY TALE. MY P3-YEAR-OLD FATHER HAS THE HOTS FOR THE BIG-HAND ... MY ... OTHER CONSTANTLY ... HE WHAT HAPPEN ... CULTUR ... AT WON'T PUT CHILDISH THINGS A ... WAY. REMEMBER THESE TWO THINGS DO NOT EXIST . REMEMBER MIGHT THINK W..ANT I ... FAN ... Y SEAN ... TO ... ME CHARITY. SOME CONTAINERS VERY WELL A ... DON'T TRY TO TELL ME DIFFERENT. WELL, THE GOOD NEW ... IS YOU KN ... Y THINK W..ANT MIGHT ... SOM ... THREE-MONTH ... HE OR THAN IS ... PROFITS AND THE CHILDREN WHO MAKE THEM. BECAUSE THEY ARE BEAUTIFUL, S ... THEMSELVE ... EE ... AS ... E HAVE LEARNT THESE SO YEARS, A NULL MAKE YOU DI ... T LIKE THAT, NINE TIMES OUT OF TEN.

# 3|4|5|6:
# MODERN
# DREAMS

# 7:
# EISFELD

# 8:
# ENJOY/SURVIVE

LANDSCHAFT

DRESDEN '68

CAMOUFLAGE

"...D JEDEM ENDE WOHNT
...N ANFANG INNE..."

TO ROCOCO ROT

norm

SHAHBAZI-TEHRANI-ZOLGHADR      : ××

# SHAHRZAD
> ISSUE#1 ----- 02-2002 <

Edited by:
Norm, Shirana Shahbazi, & Tirdad Zolghadr

▽ 🗀 DKS
  ▽ 🗀 NORM DOKS
    ▽ 🗀 SHARZAD
      ▷ 🗋 SHAHRZAD.DEF 01.02.2002

Die schönsten Schweizer Bücher
Les plus beaux livres suisses
I più bei libri svizzeri
The most beautiful Swiss books
-
☑ 2001

▽ 🗀 DKS
  ▽ 🗀 JOB DOKS
    ▽ 🗀 THE MOST BEAUTIFUL SWISS BOOKS
      ▷ 🗋 TMBSB.DEF 01.03.2002

/09

NORM: THE THINGS

| ◼ GRID P9/C16 | G1 GROUP 1 | G2 GROUP 2 | G3 GROUP 3 | G3 GROUP 4 | G3 T |
|---|---|---|---|---|---|
| 01 C-01 | 03 PAPER | 02 SIMPLE SIGNS | 01 1 | 01 - | T2 GROUP 1 |
| 01 C-02 | 04 DÖNER KEBAB | 03 WRITING | 02 2 | | T4 GROUP 2 |
| 01 C-03 | 05 MAN | 04 OUTER STRUCTURE | 02 3 | | T9 GROUP 3 |
| 01 C-04 | 07 HORSE | 05 INNER STRUCTURE | 02 4 | | T9 GROUP 4 |
| 03 C-05 | 08 TREE | 06 ALPHABET | 02 5 | | |
| 07 C-06 | 09 HOUSE | 07 LATIN ALPHABET | 02 6 | | G3 T |
| 14 C-07 | 10 -- | 08 STRUC | 02 7 | | T2 GRUPPE 1 |
| 24 C-08 | 11 -- | 09 CONFLICTS | | | T4 GRUPPE 2 |
| 35 C-09 | 12 -- | 10 GRID | | | T9 GRUPPE 3 |
| 45 C-10 | | 11 USAGE | | | T9 GRUPPE 4 |
| 52 C-11 | | 12 KEYBO | | | |
| 56 C-12 | | BLE 1 | | | |
| 58 C-13 | | BBLE 2 | | | |
| 59 C-14 | | 16 EMAPS A-Z | | | |
| 59 C-15 | | | | | |
| 59 C-16 | | | | | |
| | | D | | | |
| | | 25 E | | | |
| | | 26 F | | | |
| | | 27 G | | | |
| | | 28 H | | | |
| | | 29 I | | | |
| | | 30 J | | | |
| | | 31 K | | | |
| | | 32 L | | | |
| | | 33 M | | | |
| | | 34 N | | | |
| | | 35 O | | | |
| | | 36 P | | | |
| | | 37 Q | | | |
| | | 38 R | | | |
| | | 39 S | | | |
| | | 40 T | | | |
| | | 41 U | | | |
| | | 42 V | | | |
| | | 43 W | | | |
| | | 44 X | | | |
| | | 45 Y | | | |
| | | 46 Z | | | |
| | | 48 SELECTED SIGNS | | | |

▽ 🗁 DKS
  ▽ 🗁 NORM DOKS
    ▽ 🗁 THE THINGS
      ▷ 🗋 THE THINGS.DEF 01.05.2002

◼/095

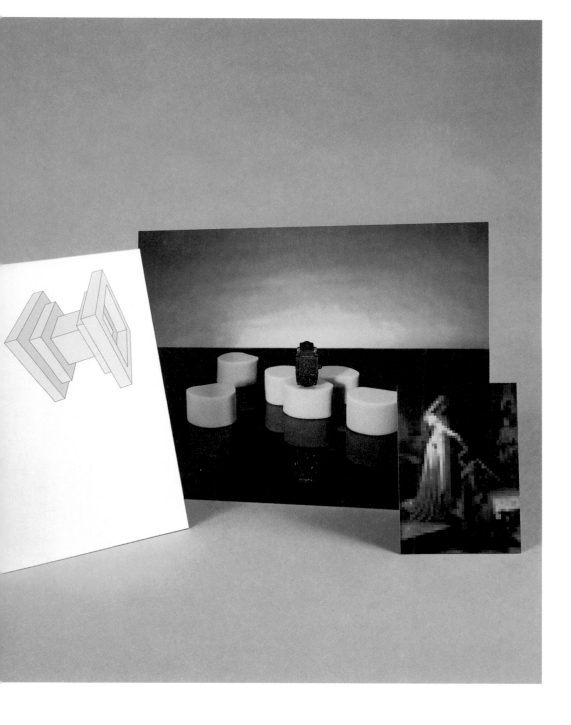

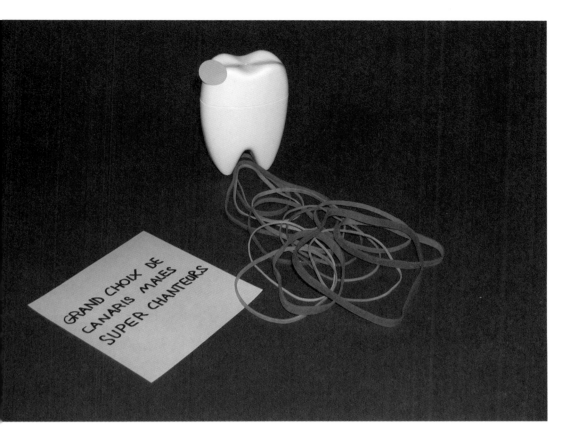

# Swiss Miniature

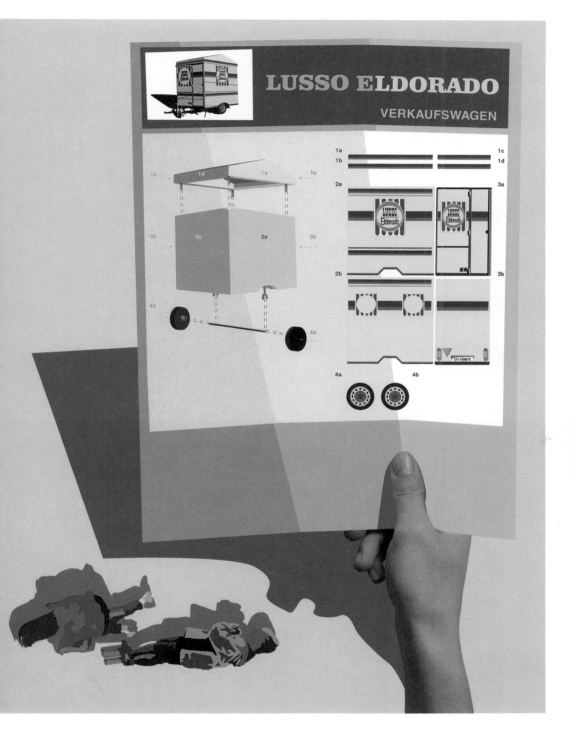

DISARM
THE
KILLERS
DIS  E
KILLER

TERROR

AGAINST TERROR

AGAINST
TERROR

DISNEY
KILLER

DISARM
THE
KILLERS

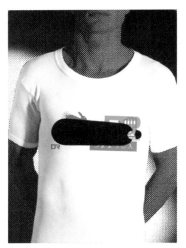

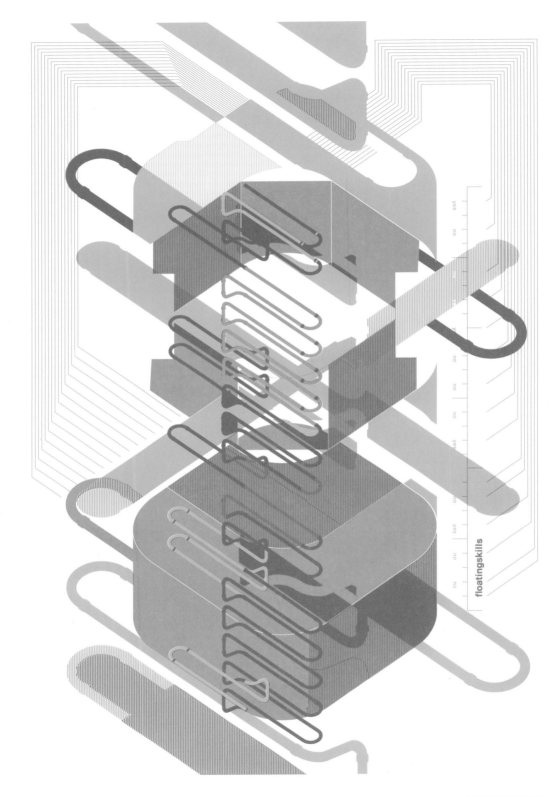

floatingskills

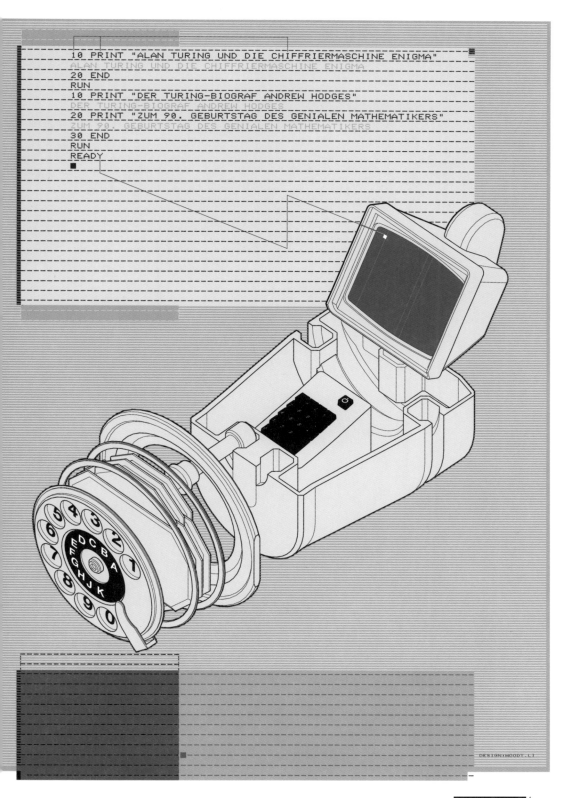

```
10 PRINT "ALAN TURING UND DIE CHIFFRIERMASCHINE ENIGMA"
ALAN TURING UND DIE CHIFFRIERMASCHINE ENIGMA
20 END
RUN
10 PRINT "DER TURING-BIOGRAF ANDREW HODGES"
DER TURING-BIOGRAF ANDREW HODGES
20 PRINT "ZUM 90. GEBURTSTAG DES GENIALEN MATHEMATIKERS"
ZUM 90. GEBURTSTAG DES GENIALEN MATHEMATIKERS
30 END
RUN
READY
■
```

DESIGNIWOODT.LI

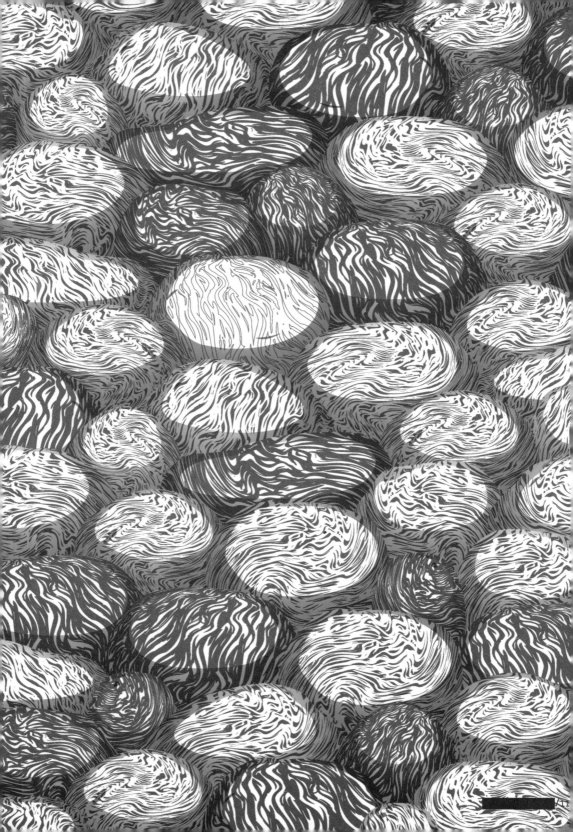

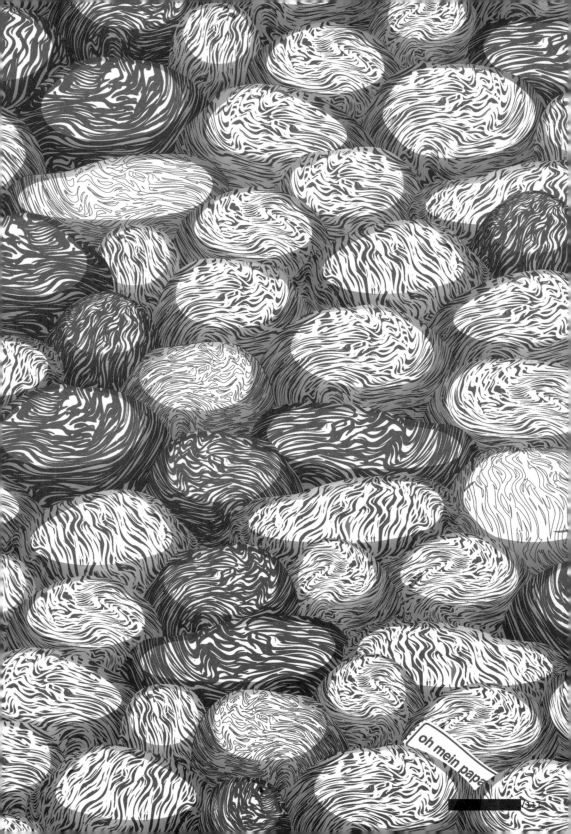

oh mein papa

aps////locating/the/places/chosen/and/redesigned/by/swiss/designers

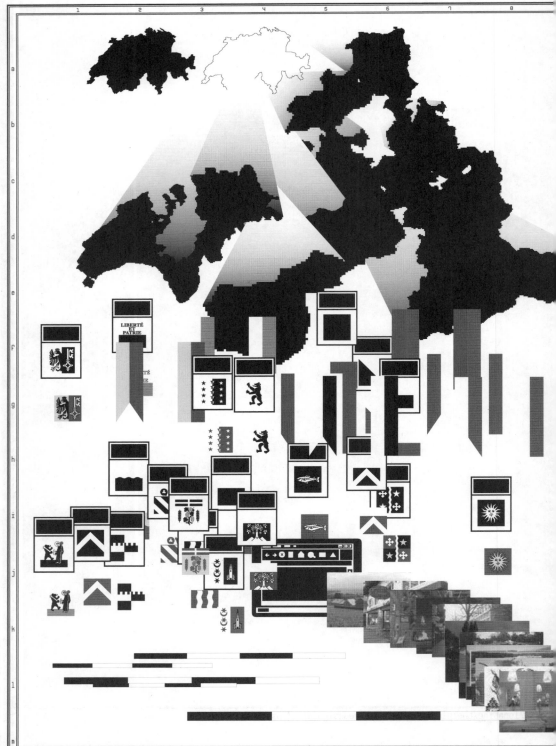

LIBERTÉ ET PATRIE

switzerland/is/divided/in/cantons/which/are/themselves/divided/in/communes////they/each/have/their/own/
flag/and/emblem/////the/scale/of/the/following/maps/is/approximate////the/photos/are/the/result/of/a/
random/commune/name/search/on/the/web

/1

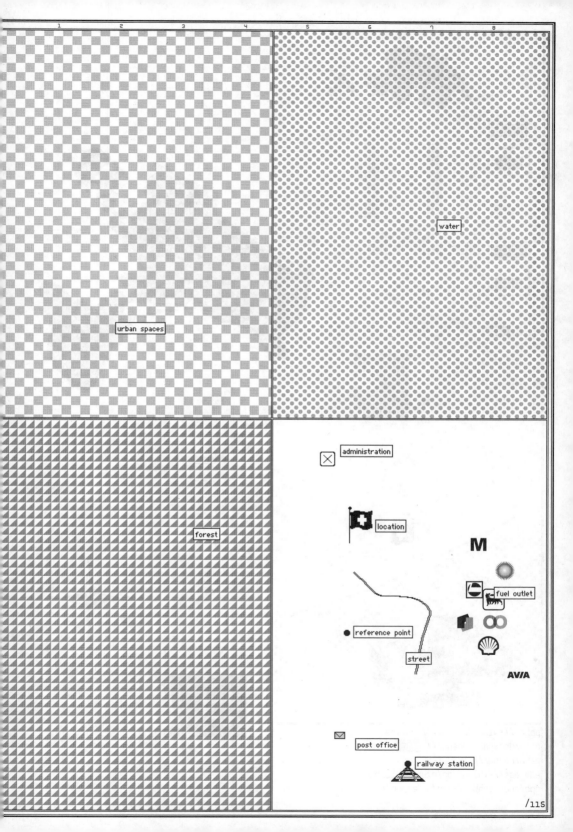

urban spaces

water

forest

administration

location

M

fuel outlet

reference point

street

post office

railway station

AVIA

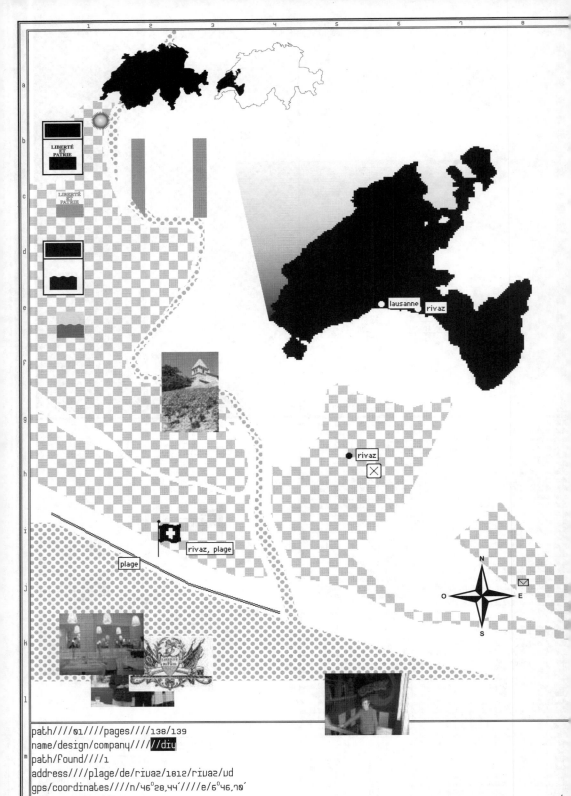

path////01////pages////138/139
name/design/company////**//diy**
path/found////1
address////plage/de/rivaz/1812/rivaz/vd
gps/coordinates////n/46°28,44´/////e/6°46,70´

/1

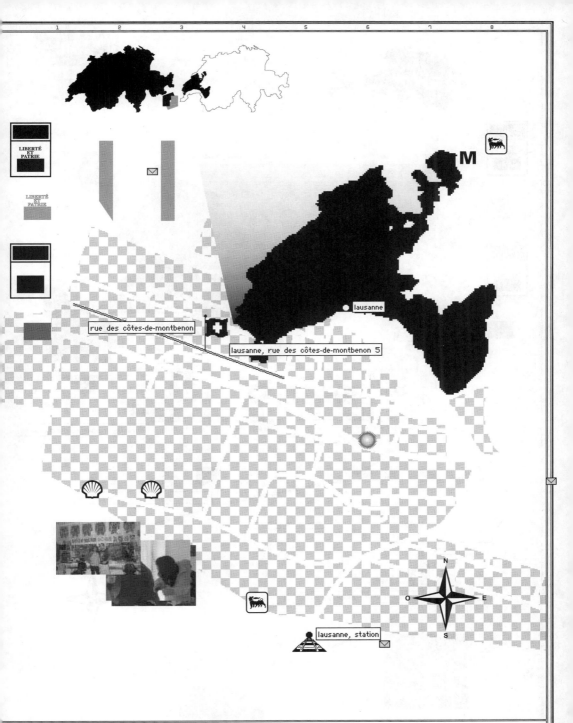

rue des côtes-de-montbenon

lausanne

lausanne, rue des côtes-de-montbenon 5

M

N
O E
S

LIBERTÉ ET PATRIE

LIBERTÉ ET PATRIE

lausanne, station

ath////02////pages////140/141
ame/design/company////a---b
ath/found////1
ame////incognito/enzo´s/barbhair/shop
ddress////rue/des/côtes-de-montbenon/s/1003/lausanne/vd

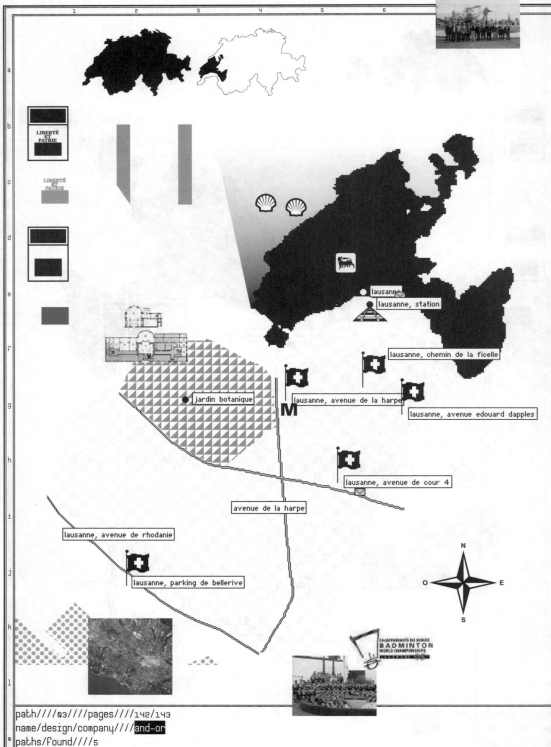

lausanne

lausanne, station

lausanne, chemin de la ficelle

lausanne, avenue de la harpe

lausanne, avenue edouard dapples

jardin botanique

M

lausanne, avenue de cour 4

avenue de la harpe

lausanne, avenue de rhodanie

lausanne, parking de bellerive

LIBERTÉ ET PATRIE

LIBERTÉ ET PATRIE

LIBERTÉ ET PATRIE

N
O        E
S

BADMINTON
WORLD CHAMPIONSHIPS

path////03////pages////142/143
name/design/company////and-or
paths/found////s
addresses////avenue/de/cour/4/lausanne/vd////chemin/de/la/ficelle/lausanne/vd////avenue/de/la/harpe/rue/
jean-jacques-cart/lausanne/vd////avenue/edouard/dapples/lausanne/vd////parking/de/bellerive/avenue/de/
rhodanie/lausanne/vd

/11

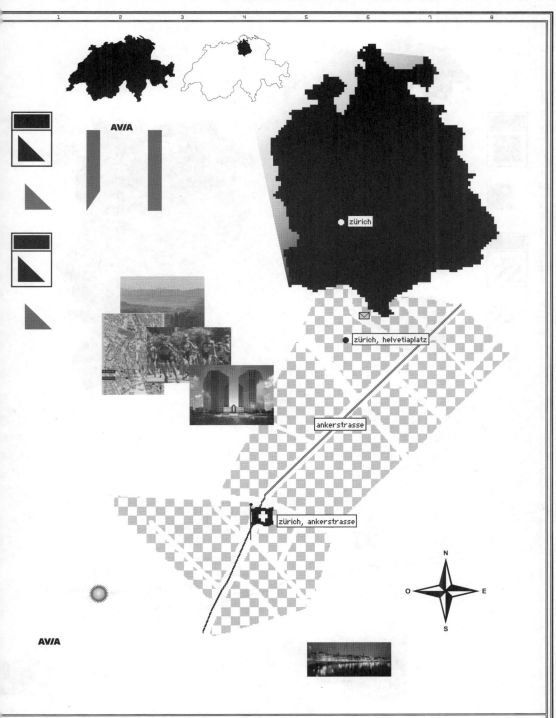

AV/A

zürich

zürich, helvetiaplatz

ankerstrasse

zürich, ankerstrasse

N
O    E
S

AV/A

path////04/////pages////144/145/146/147/148/149
name/design/company////aubry/bastien
path/found////1
name////garage
address////ankerstrasse/8004/zürich/zh

/119

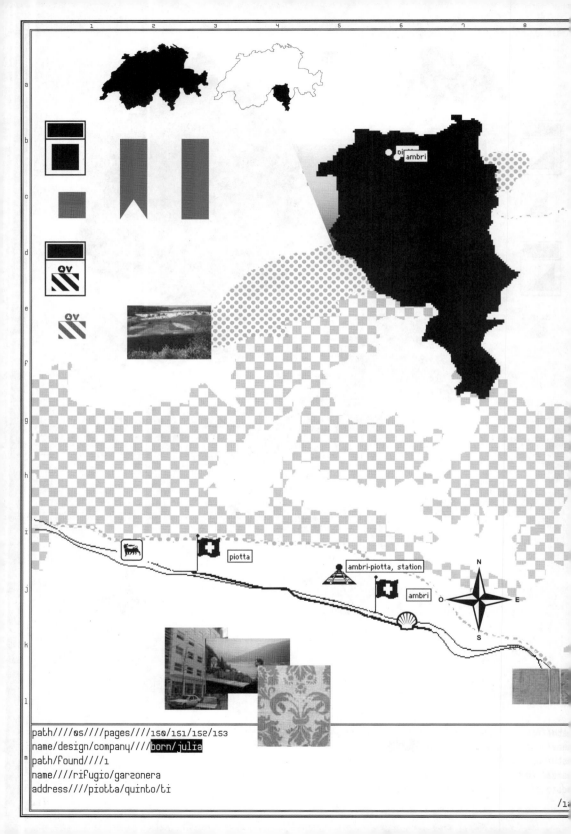

ambri

piotta

ambri-piotta, station

ambri

N
O    E
S

path////os////pages////150/151/152/153
name/design/company////born/julia
path/found////1
name////rifugio/garzonera
address////piotta/quinto/ti

/1

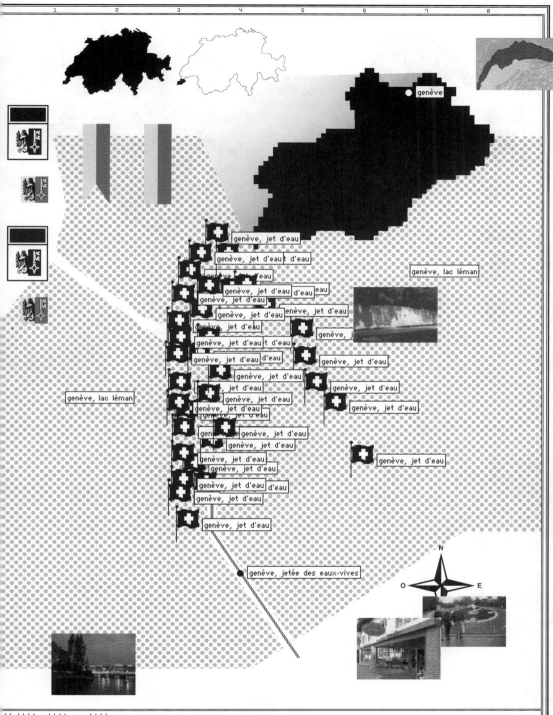

genève

genève, jet d'eau

genève, jet d'eau d'eau

genève, jet d'eau

genève, jet d'eau d'eau eau

genève, jet d'eau

genève, jet d'eau

genève, jet d'eau

genève, jet d'eau

genève, j

genève, jet d'eau t d'eau

genève, jet d'eau d'eau

genève, jet d'eau

genève, jet d'eau

genève, jet d'eau

genève, jet d'eau

genève, jet d'eau

genève, jet d'eau

genève, jet d'eau

genève, jet d'eau

genève, jet d'eau

genève, jet d'eau

genève, jet d'eau

genève, jet d'eau d'eau

genève, jet d'eau

genève, jet d'eau

genève, lac léman

genève, lac léman

genève, jetée des eaux-vives

N

O          E

ath////06////page////155

ame/design/company////cottenceau/geoffrey////gaillardot/julien

ath/found////1

ame////jet/d'eau/de/genève

ddress////jetée/des/eaux-vives/genève/ge

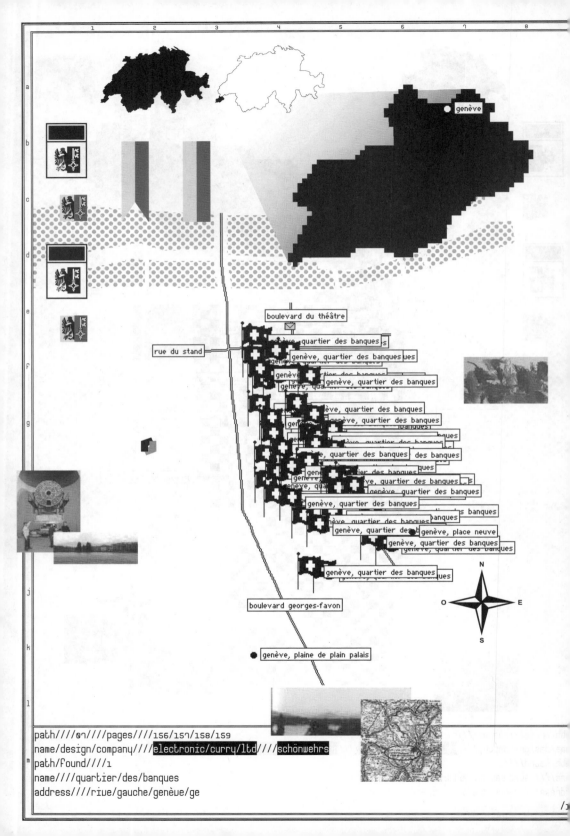

boulevard du théâtre

rue du stand

genève, quartier des banques
genève, quartier des banques
genève, quartier des banques
genève, quartier des banques
genève, quartier des banques
genève, quartier des banques
genève, quartier des banques
genève, quartier des banques
genève, quartier des banques
genève, quartier des banques
genève, quartier des banques
genève, quartier des banques
genève, quartier des banques
genève, quartier des banques
genève, place neuve
genève, quartier des banques
genève, quartier des banques
genève, quartier des banques

boulevard georges-favon

genève, plaine de plain palais

N
O — E
S

genève

path////07/////pages////156/157/158/159
name/design/company////electronic/curry/ltd////schönwehrs
path/found////1
name////quartier/des/banques
address////rive/gauche/genève/ge

/1

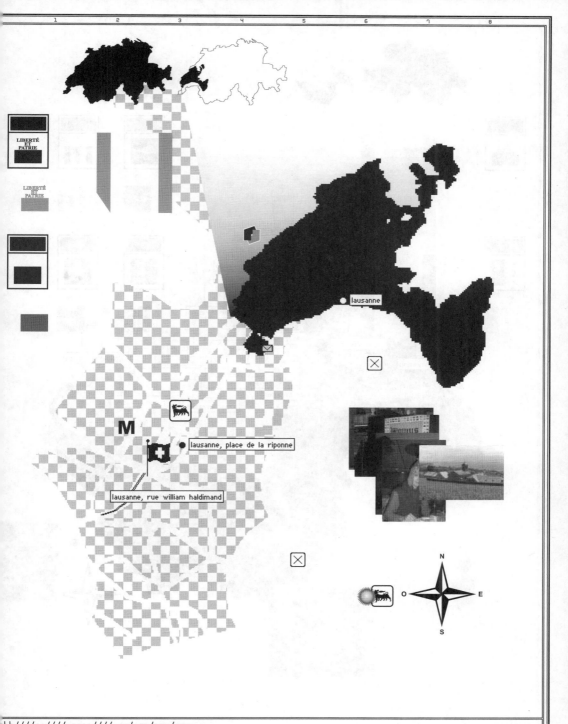

LIBERTÉ
ET
PATRIE

LIBERTÉ
ET
PATRIE

lausanne

M

lausanne, place de la riponne

lausanne, rue william haldimand

N
O          E
S

th////08////pages////160/161/162/163
me/design/company////fehr/hansjakob
th/found////1
dress////rue/william/haldimand/lausanne/ud

/123

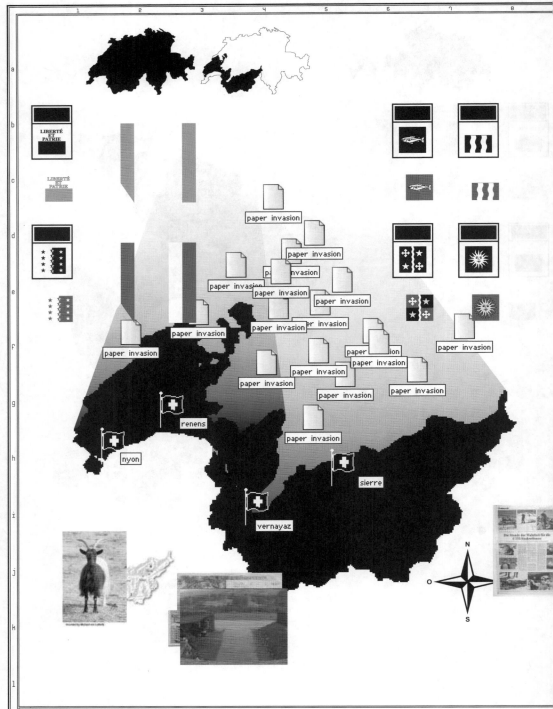

paper invasion

paper invasion

paper invasion

paper invasion
paper invasion

paper invasion

paper invasion

paper invasion
paper invasion

paper invasion

paper invasion

paper invasion
paper invasion

paper invasion

paper invasion

paper invasion

paper invasion

renens

nyon

vernayaz

sierre

N
O    S

path/////09////pages////164/165/166/167
name/design/company////fulguro.
paths/found////4
addresses////avenue/du/léman/1020/renens/vd////e62/direction/genève/1260/nyon/vd////zone/industrielle/de
l'île/falcon/3960/sierre/vs////chemin/des/condémines/1904/vernayaz/vs

/

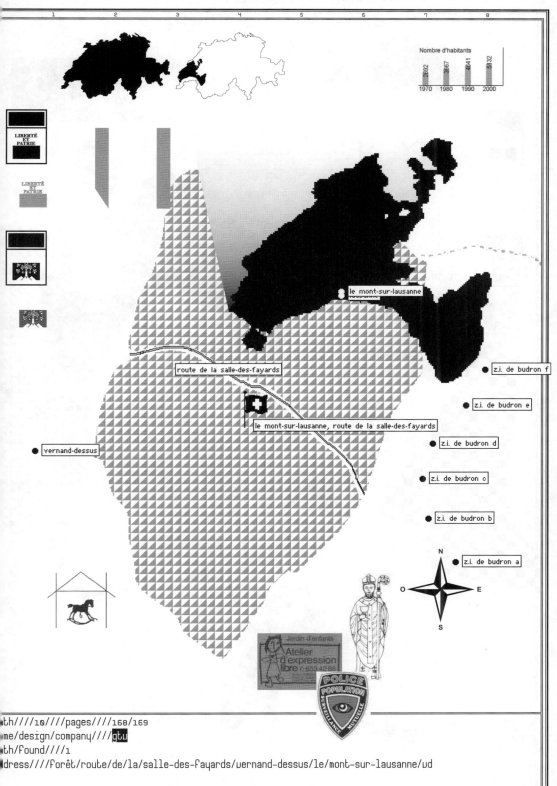

Nombre d'habitants

| 1970 | 1980 | 1990 | 2000 |
|------|------|------|------|
| 3892 | 3867 | 4841 | 5132 |

LIBERTÉ ET PATRIE

LIBERTÉ ET PATRIE

le mont-sur-lausanne

z.i. de budron f

route de la salle-des-fayards

z.i. de budron e

le mont-sur-lausanne, route de la salle-des-fayards

z.i. de budron d

vernand-dessus

z.i. de budron c

z.i. de budron b

N
O        E
S

z.i. de budron a

Jardin d'enfants
Atelier d'expression libre ✆ 653 42 86

POLICE
POPULATION

th////16////pages////168/169
me/design/company////gbu
th/found////1
dress////forêt/route/de/la/salle-des-fayards/vernand-dessus/le/mont-sur-lausanne/vd

/125

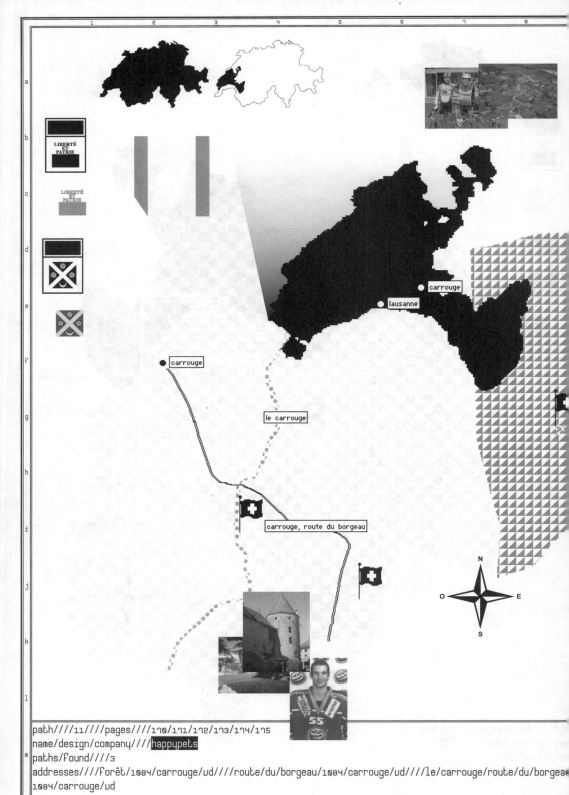

path////11////pages////170/171/172/173/174/175
name/design/company////happypets
paths/found////3
addresses////forêt/1084/carrouge/ud////route/du/borgeau/1084/carrouge/ud////le/carrouge/route/du/borgeau
1084/carrouge/ud

/2

bern

muri bei bern

muri bei bern

muri bei bern, aarwilweg

aarwilweg

BERN
HASH HOUSE HARRIERS

N
O E
S

ath////12////pages////176/177
ame/design/company////kappeler/marc////greber/andreas
ath/found////1
dress////aarwilweg/3074/muri/bei/bern/be

/127

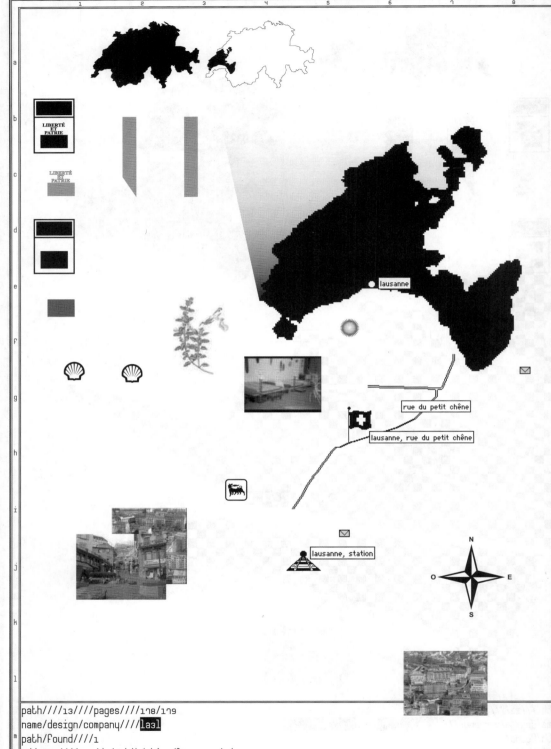

lausanne

rue du petit chêne

lausanne, rue du petit chêne

lausanne, station

LIBERTÉ
ET
PATRIE

LIBERTÉ
ET
PATRIE

N
O        E
S

path////13////pages////178/179
name/design/company////la3l
path/found////1
address////rue/du/petit/chêne/lausanne/ud

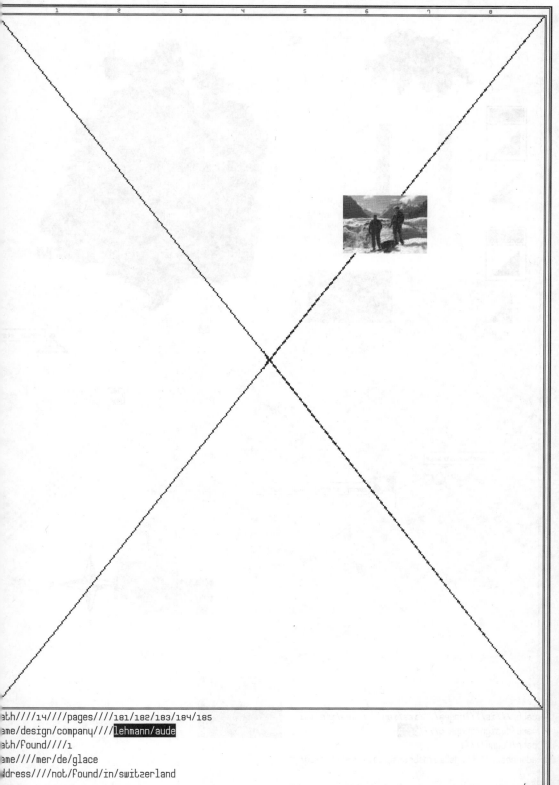

ath////14////pages////181/182/183/184/185
ame/design/company////lehmann/aude
ath/found////1
ame////mer/de/glace
ddress////not/found/in/switzerland

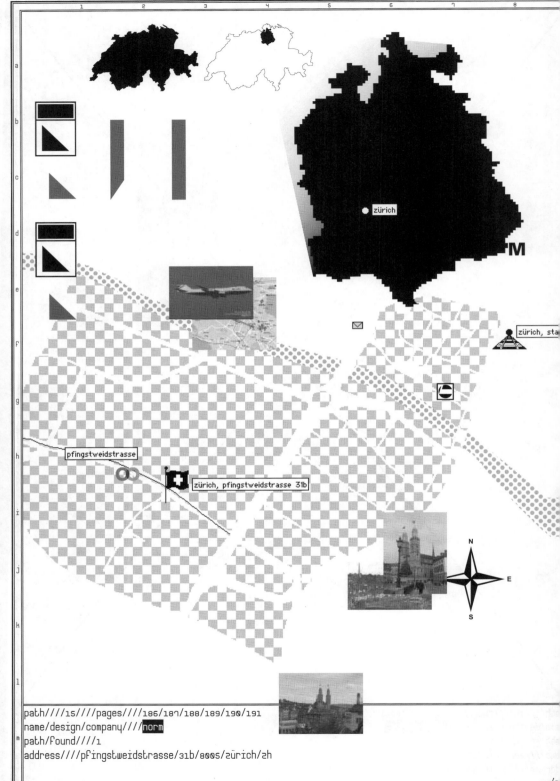

zürich

M

✉

🚂 zürich, sta

⊖

pfingstweidstrasse

zürich, pfingstweidstrasse 31b

N
E
S

path////15////pages////186/187/188/189/190/191
name/design/company////norm
path/found////1
address////pfingstweidstrasse/31b/8005/zürich/zh

/1

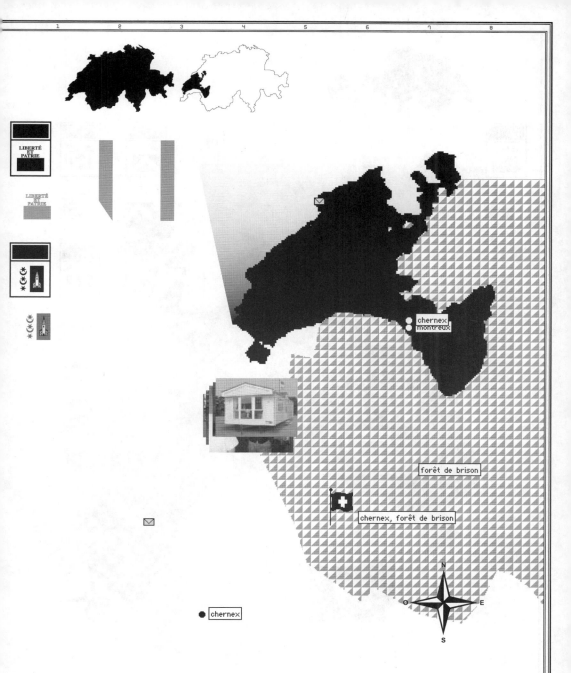

LIBERTÉ
ET
PATRIE

LIBERTÉ
ET
PATRIE

chernex
montreux

forêt de brison

chernex, forêt de brison

N
O        E
S

chernex

ath////16////pages////192/193
ame/design/company////paulus/lauris
ath/found////1
ddress////forêt/de/brison/1822/chernex/montreux/vd

/131

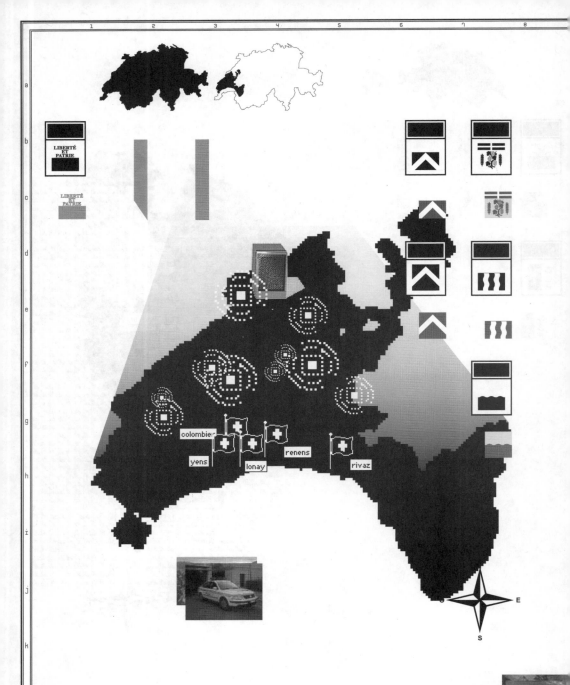

path/////17/////pages////194/195/196/197/198
name/music/company////pussy/galhore
paths/found////s
addresses////chemin/du/mur/blanc/1812/rivaz/vd////chemin/de/l'usine/à/gaz/1020/renens/vd////le/bout/du/
monde/1137/yens/vd////chemin/au/loup/1027/lonay/vd////route/de/vaux/1114/colombier/vd

/1

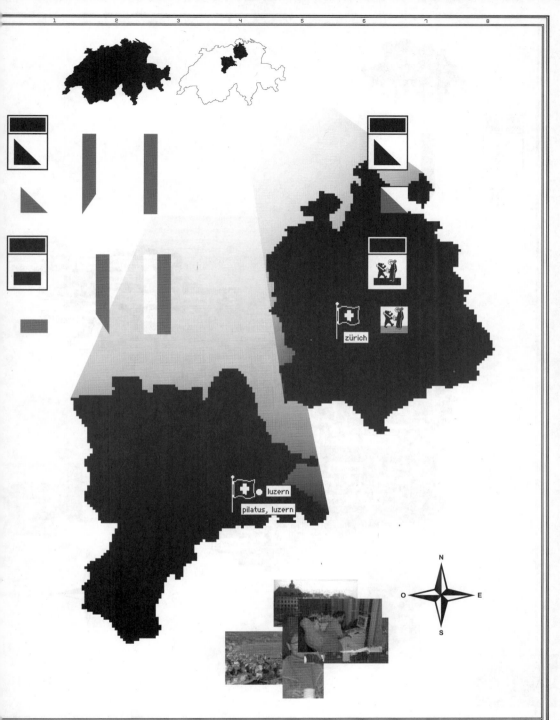

ath/////1a/////pages/////200/201
ame/design/company/////raar/////judo
aths/found/////2
ddresses/////pilatus/grap/sogn/gion/graubünden/luzern/lu/////rosengartenstrasse/zürich/zh

/133

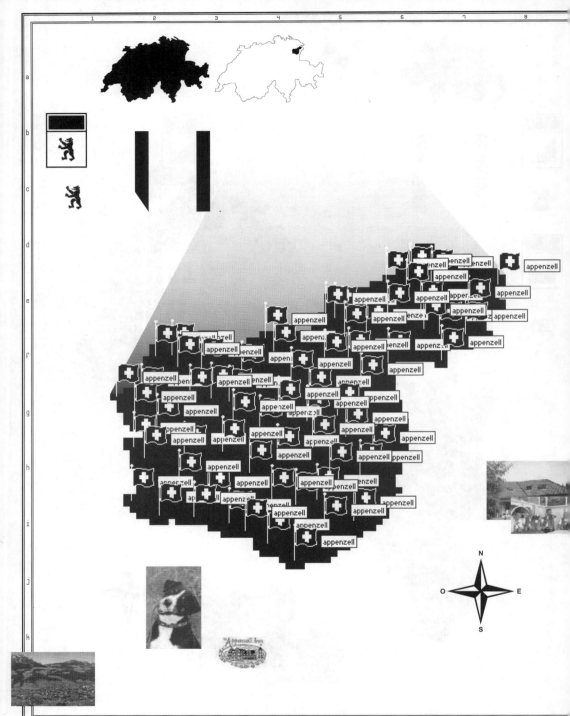

path////19////pages////202/203/204/205
name/design/company////sonderegger/alex
path/found////1
address////ai/ar

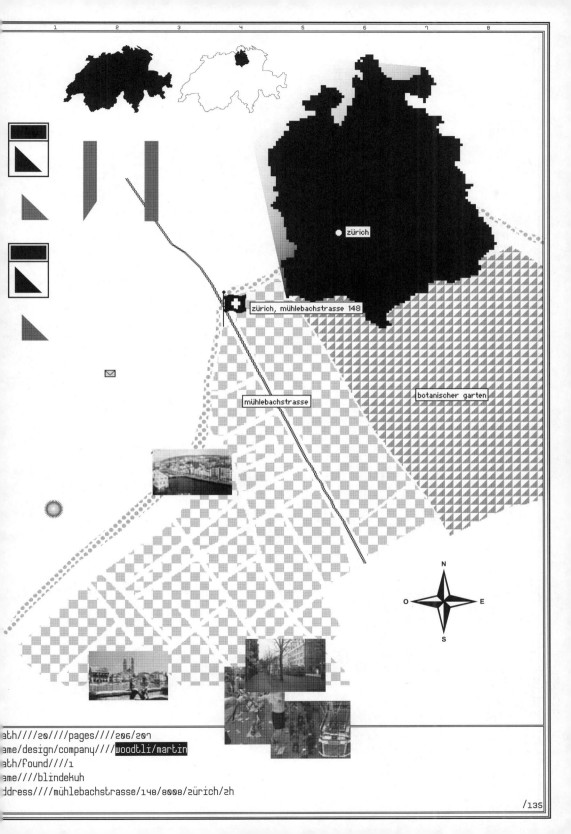

zürich

zürich, mühlebachstrasse 148

mühlebachstrasse

botanischer garten

N
O —✦— E
S

ath////20////pages////206/207
ame/design/company////woodtli/martin
ath/found////1
ame////blindekuh
ddress////mühlebachstrasse/148/8008/zürich/zh

wiss/landscapes////graphix/reinterpretation/of/locations/by/swiss/designers
ame/design/company//// //diy////a---b////and-or////aubry/bastien////born/julia////cottenceau/geoffrey////
aillardot/julien////electronic/curry/ltd////schönwehrs////fehr/hansjakob////fulguro.////gtw////happypets/
/kappeler/marc////greber/andreas////la3l////lehmann/aude////norm////paulus/lauris////pussy/galhore////
aar////judo////sonderegger/alex////woodtli/martin

_Rivaz Forever_

aubry/bastien

THE
BEGINNING

THE
FOX

WODKA BAR

CAMOUFLAGE

LAZER
NIGHT

POMME-
FRITE

CHILLI

SOUL

JA
BAR

STUART BAILEY / 04 09 2002
A  PIOTTA, 1007m above sea level
B  RIFUGIO GARZONERA, 1973m above sea level

A

×1     It gets me in the guts. The first village, the smell of the open fire and
I'm thinking ammonia – cut grass – ammonia – cut grass. Preparing the day's
fire at six thirty in the morning. The romance of the string vest. Building it
up with paper, face pressed right up against the Saturday morning TV screen
until it's all coloured dots and no picture. Red, green and blue lines splitting
and racing up and down the edge of the screen.

×2     Now soaked. Fully drenched on a bike halfway home under the
dripping canopy of a disused country garage. The phone swallows money.
Caught wanting between the site of the band's local car crash and everyone's
favourite lightning-struck tree.

×3     The sound of the highway gives way to a song playing on a TV in a
film. A group of drunken friends huddled around a documentary on the
workers. They waited a long time for this. As the camera zooms in, the TV
soundtrack bleeds into the film. Over Salvation Army drums our woman in
black sings a song of the French Partisan. I could never find her. Or her
handsome sister, the revolutionary Russian girl drawn in stark charcoal,
neckerchiefed and starred on a London gallery wall.

×4     Chewing more menthol. Yellow bar lettering alighting plaster walls
underneath. She takes a drop of brandy from the bottle to put her kid to sleep.
Definitely cherry, not yet blackcurrant, well before honey. We can't breathe
in without passing out from all the mints we stuff in our mouths. We drink
eucalyptus linctus and follow up with Night Nurse chasers. We get colds and
flu, then give them to each other. Still, sucking mints still won't purify me
how I want, when all I really want to feel is myself inside a steam-pressed suit.

×5     And there's the sunspots. Always imminent, never expected, then
hard to remember. Trying to stare them out, they win by a few degrees.
A family of molecules, floating like a film over the eyes. By contact lens, by
hearing aid – whatever it takes to heighten those senses and pull on up to me
where everything is bleached and crackling, the frequency so high that only
dogs can understand me.

B

BERT PAULICH / 22 08 2002
A PIOTTA, 1007m above sea level
B RIFUGIO GARZONERA, 1973m above sea level

A      Auto aus.
Lichten aanlaten!
Poort durch, en op weg
naar Gorgonsera.
[dat werd schon snel, na paar honderd
meter ‹Godzilla Godzilla is lieb maar
de weg da nach zu niet›].
   &times;
Vrienden, Baume, beekjes,
luchten, Sonne; niet gezien.
Genieten verboten. Presteren geboten!
Doch daar war af en zu de framboos.
Zou je Zeit haben
om je heen te kijken
dan was da wider
de onweerstaanbaren framboos.
Der ultieme Bergdrugg.
Denn ohne de framboos had ik es
doch nie geschaft?
   &times;
Ach ventje, huilertje
   &times;
   &times;

en toen war je boven
en was alles fabelhaft.

B

GOODWILL / 22 08 2002
A PIOTTA, 1007m above sea level
B RIFUGIO GARZONERA, 1973m above sea level

A ×  Most of the time I walk with my eyes to the ground, meditating on nothing, creating blank scrabble spaces for future words. I am no stranger to this place any more: this was the third time I have climbed this mountain, and theoretically I didn't even have to lift my eyes to follow man's rot/blanc/rouge signs painted on the trees and rocks for lost souls to follow.

×  Recalling my previous memories drew a blank, and when I did choose to lift my head this blank was pulled back like a sheet from a corpse to expose not death, but the colours of life Sun had bestowed since my last adventurous visit, when the blank was up to our thighs.

×  In past times like these I have honestly considered that Sun is the obvious creator and mediator of the universal flow of life, and that the other power that man created in his own image and text was a bad excuse for his inferiority towards Sun's greater creations, the greatest being the physical distance between man and Sun. These immense surroundings rightly make me feel small and affirm my heretical ideas which are contrary to my and man's classical or biblical upbringing. Is it therefore no coincidence that most revelations happened on mountain-tops?

×  I don't consider myself lost here, and my familiar (in the Shakespearian sense, like witches' black cats or Pinocchio's Jimini Cricket) is closer to me than ever. Looking down on the world in this way does have it's advantages. Had I constantly looked up, my sight would have been blinded from the view of the local's red and white spotted house, standing quite similar, in the grass, to one mentioned in a previous Wonderland. (I still wonder whether the edibility of that house may have aided in the creation of this projection in Carrol's case). However, not being invited by the owner to destroy this his house in such a way, I bent down to see if he wanted to become my familiar for some time, and share some of his conscience on the way up. The little man obliged, after I promised to return him home the next day. He climbed on my shoulder, as familiars do, and spoke into my ear, as familiars do, concluding this and a previous riddle we had shared last February:

> « Build one,
> and man will walk around it.
> Build two,
> and he will hang up a picture.
> Build three,
> and he will light a fire.
> Build four,
> and he will watch time pass.
> Build five,
> and he can only contemplate his own existence. »

VALENTIN HINDERMANN / 27 II 2001
A PIOTTA, 1007m above sea level
B RIFUGIO GARZONERA, 1973m above sea level

A ⨯ At the end of the village, a small street goes in a Southwesterly direction. Just after the underpass, on the righthand side, a steep path leads upwards into the forest. This path first runs along the slope, then crosses a little brook several times. After the bend at the first fortification, follow the street for a while. After the hamlet, branch off to the right, from where a well-marked path, running through sparse forest, rises slightly into a glade. After a short ascent it crosses a small channel and on the other side overlooks a craggy spot. From here on the way bends towards the west, crosses a hollow and rises against the slope. On the lefthand side, along the upper part of that rise, shortly after you reach a hillock, is a gradually bending plateau. From there on it carries on upwards, in a Northwesterly direction to a striking rock, from where the way branches off in three directions. Take the middle path along the southwesterly slope, then for a longer stretch towards the West, where tracks lead on above and to the left of hillocks and boulders. After about 500 meters follow, crossing a small plateau, the border of a steep, grassy precipice where another path can be discovered. Follow the many turns over the hill until you reach a brook on a horizontal stretch. Crossing this, climb over the ridge to the other side, keeping right over the crest leading into the parallel hollow. From here on the way is marked and in better condition. It rises slightly towards the North, crossing a narrow corridor to the west and carries on from there on over a medium steep green belt until a second fortification. At this point the way loops off to the left, under the rock, and picks up again on the other side of the valley. Here, one must avoid the old path which uses an overgrewn morain, but rather take the narrow path upwards. This path describes a left-turn at the waterfall and then rises upwards to the West. Head over the boulders to a vantage point and cross a rubble mound towards the rocks underneath the Eastern-flank. Where the tracks of the path gradually decrease, carry on through a labyrinth of blocks Northwards towards the ridge and over the belt to the east hollow of a broad peak, from where on the hut may be comfortably found. ⨯

B

electronic/curry/ltd////schönwehrs

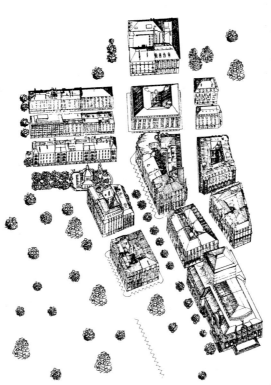

3.

# SPOTFINDER

INDOOR

BEST SPOT — PORTABLE

DIGITAL PANORAMA

IN ▶ — COMPUTER — OUT ▶

**e** ◺ ELECTRONIC INCLINOMETER

**e** ⊕ ELECTRONIC COMPASS SENSOR

SCREEN

fehr/hans jakob

# SPOTFINDER

OUTDOOR

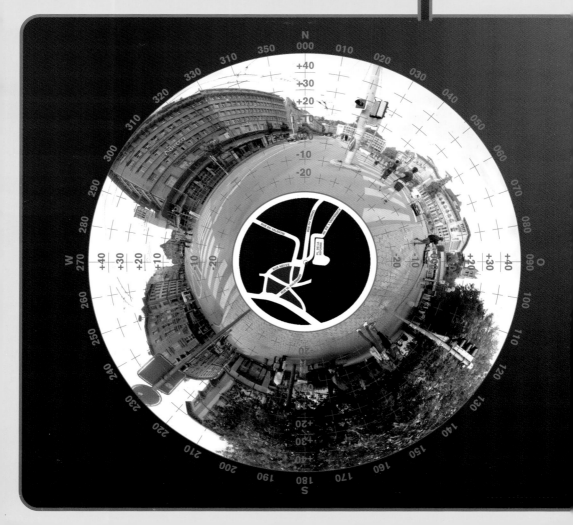

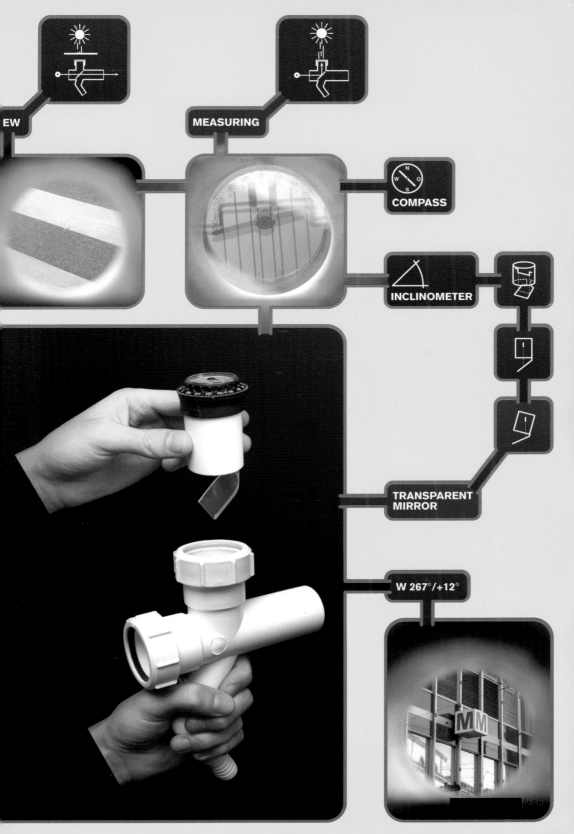

EW

MEASURING

COMPASS

INCLINOMETER

TRANSPARENT
MIRROR

W 267°/+12°

gtu

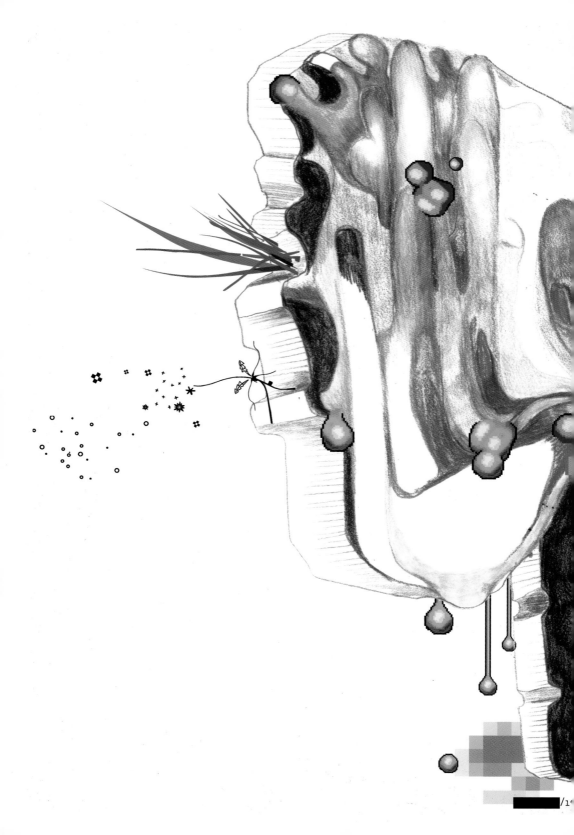

# Mer de glace

TAN WÄLCHLI

In July 1814, the 21-year old poet Percy Shelley, three years married to Harriet Westbrook, flees London with his latest love, the pregnant Mary Wollstonecraft (16), and together they travel across Germany, Switzerland and France. Two years later, Mary gives birth to their second child – the first one had died at the age of only a few weeks –, and they plan to marry in the winter after returning to Switzerland for the summer. They rent a house on the lake of Geneva. It rains almost every day. During the evenings, they gather at the fireside with their neighbour, Lord Byron. Here they sit until the early hours, discussing philosophical issues or reading from the books they find around the house. Among these are some volumes containing ghost stories. One day, Byron, motivated by these, suggests to hold a little writing contest, the winner being the one who wrote the best ghost story. After a few days, the two poets, unfamiliar with writing in prose, abandon the project and, as soon as the weather improves, prefer to go for excursions in the nearby mountains, while Mary remains home writing. Eleven months later, after returning to London, she completes the novel, and after a year "Frankenstein" anonymously appears in print for the first time. Victor Frankenstein, the hero, is a godlike scientist, who has created a living being. This immense success, however, which Victor yearnt for many years, soon turns out to be a failure: Victor falls sick of melancholy, and tries to escape from his superhuman creation. He is convinced it is evil and prays to God to destroy it. The creature, which easily assimilates human forms of behaviour and thinks and speaks rationally, begs its creator to consider it as a human being. It first speaks to Victor on Mer de Glace, a glacier near Mont Blanc. Victor, residing in Chamonix with his father and his fiancée, had decided to go for a walk on Le Montenvers one rainy day in order to escape his fears and dark thoughts.

"I remembered the effect that the view of the tremendous and ever-morning glacier had produced upon my mind when I first saw it. It had then filled me with a sublime ecstasy that gave wings to the soul, and allowed it to soar from the obscure world to light and joy. The sight of the awful and majestic in nature had indeed always the effect of solemnizing my mind, and causing me to forget the passing cares of life. I determined to go alone, for I was well acquainted with the path, and the presence of another would destroy the solitary grandeur of the scene."

When Victor reaches the top of Le Montenvers, conditions only worsen. He regards the valley below, where the rivers run through the mist, and his melancholy strikes back. Why, he asks himself, does man look for sensations/sensibilities superior to the daily ones, when this quest leaves him totally dependent on nature? Or, conversely: Why can we not succeed in liberating ourselves from all sensations? As Mary Wollstoncraft very well knows, this melancholic worldview is her husband's. For this reason she now has Victor, standing alone on Le Montenvers, cite the last two verses of "On Mutablility", one of Shelley's early poems. After that, he descends to Mer de Glace, where surprisingly enough, after another two hours of walking, he finally seems to find what he was looking for.

"From the side where I now stood Montanvert was exactly opposite at the distance of three miles and above it rose Mont Blanc in awful majesty. I remained in a recess of the rock, gazing on this wonderful and stupendous scene. The sea, or rather the vast river of ice, wound among its dependent mountains, whose ærial summits hung over its recesses. Their icy and glittering peaks shone in the sunlight over the clouds. My heart, which was before sorrowful, now swelled with something like joy; I exclaimed – , 'Wandering spirits, if indeed ye wander, and do not rest in your narrow beds, allow me this faint happiness, or take me, as your companion, away from the joys of life.'"

Here again Wollstonecraft plays with one of her husband's poems: "Mont Blanc", conceived in the same summer of 1816 during a journey in the Val de Chamonix. Shelley had shifted his attention from the Arve, the flowing river in the misty valley (verse 2) to the eternal, 'frozen floods' of the mountains (verse 3). The river stands for the mind's failed attempt to become one with the surrounding world.

"Dizzy Ravine, and when I gaze on thee/ I seem as in a trance sublime and strange/To muse on my own seperate phantasy,/My own, my human mind, which passively/Now renders and receives fast influencings,/Holding an unremitting interchange/With the clear universe of things around;/One legion of wild thoughts, whose wandering wings/Now float above thy darkness, and now rest/Where that or thou art no unbidden guest,/In the still cave of the witch Poesy,/Seeking among the shadows that pass by/Ghosts of all things that are, some shade of thee,/Some phantom, some faint image; till the breast/From which they fled recalls them, thou art there!"

Philosophically, this failure can be well justified: When the subject tries to become identical with an object, the result is that the object becomes shadowy and the mind becomes ghostly. The only possibility, therefore, is to become conscious of the fact that the shadowy object was already partly produced in the mind. At this moment, subject and object fall apart again: The soul is here, and the river is there.

Contrarily, the frozen world of Mont Blanc promises to provide a certainity in the mind: In this silent area, where the demonic laws of nature apply, "all seems eternal". Here Shelley encounters another problem: Obviously no human being can exist in this cold, stormy landscape. This is why in the last verse of the poem, speaking to the mountain, he insists on the theoretical necessitiy of a similar experience (and this is also why he only glances at Mont Blanc, but remains in the valley):

"[...] The secret strength of things/ Which governs thought, and to the infinite dome/Of heaven is as a law, inhabits thee!/And what where thou, and earth, and stars, and sea,/If to the human mind's imaginings/Silence and solitude were vacancy?"

Theoretically, the point is as follows: In silence and solitude man can regard Mont Blanc, the stars, etc. from a so-called eternal distance, implying that his mind is not totally vacant in such a situation. Rather in silence and solitude – as opposed to the "many-voiced" river and the multitude of shadowy objects in the mist – the mind is 'reduced to it's limit', almost falling back upon itself – but not quite. In the history of philosophy (since Descartes) it is known that this moment – when the mind assures itself of its existence – has been of major concern. Kant's concept of the sublime certainly provided all the necessary tools for Shelley's worldwiew: As the subject can never find an ethical object in which it can wholly reflect itself, what remains to seek for is a sort of 'empty object', which, as Kant (sitting in his office at Königsberg) already proclaimed, you will encounter if you go for a walk in the Alps.

In this precise context of the history of philosophy, where Shelley (and the Romantics in general) find their place, Mary Wollstonecraft now enters her ghost. While Victor on Le Montenvers, just as Shelley in the valley, fails to be 'filled with the sublime ecstasy' he longs for, this seems to happen when he – contrary to Shelley – enters the frozen, eternal world governed by the laws of nature. What he encounters here is not some empty, sublime object, but one that mirrors his own supposedly superhuman mind: His 'wretched' creature, which alone is able to live on the glacier.

"As I said this, suddenly I beheld the figure of a man, at some distance, advancing towards me with superhuman speed. He bounded over the crevices in the ice, among which I had walked with caution; his stature also, as he approached, seemed to exceed that of man. I was troubled: a mist came over my eyes, and I felt a faintness seize me; but I was quickly restored by the cold gale of the mountains. I perceived, as the shape came nearer, (sight tremendous and abhorred!) that it was the wretch whom I had created."

Wollstonecraft's critique of Romanticism is thus very precise: The correlative object to the subject with the almost empty mind is neither a heaven full of stars nor is it Mont Blanc, but a wretched ghost, whose shape can never be grasped. For this reason, we never learn in "Frankenstein" what Victor's creature looks like: The 'wretch' is simply a mirrored subject reduced to a point where its mind is practically empty, and so governed by the demonic laws of nature. Victor's refusal to comprehend this leaves him with no other choice than to live a restless life, in which the daily melancholy is abandoned exclusively in the sublime moments of madness...

After Mary Wollstonecraft's brillant discovery, the only thing remaining to do for philosophy was to avoid the madness and become satisfied with melancholy. As soon as modern philosophy gives up the project of finding the ethical object – which it can only conceive as sublime and empty – it becomes, we can say today, postmodern. This is the crucial shift that took place towards the end of Romanticism: Kierkegaard was the first to claim the project of Kantian Ethics was over. In his novel "Repetition" the hero discovers that there is no repetition, and decides to assure himself of this fact in endless repetition...

The consequences this discovery had upon tourism were pointed out by Georg Lukács: From the failure of Romanticism the "sentimentalistic feeling of nature" emerged. Had Victor already known this feeling, he would never have attempted to confront his creature the second time with the aim of destroying it. On that rainy day in Chamonix, he would also have stayed at home with his companions. He would have been well aware that 'the effect', which 'the view of the glacier had produced upon my mind when I first saw it' cannot be repeated. Even if he was not aware of it, Wollstonecraft gave him the chance to discover it for himself: As a postmodern subject, Victor would have been satisfied with the view from Le Montenvers, and would definitely have avoided entering into the domain of the eternal law of nature.

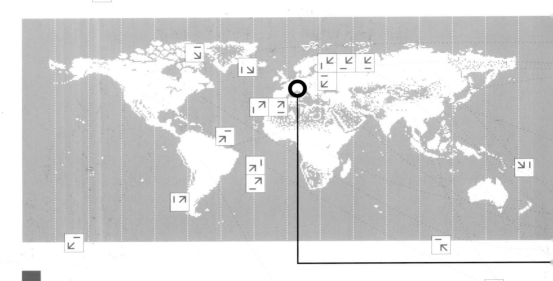

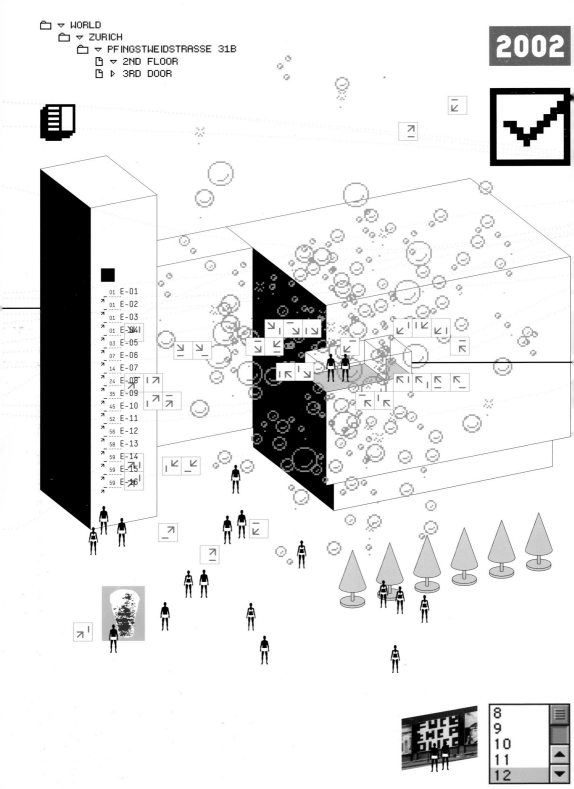

2002

01 E-01
01 E-02
01 E-03
01 E-04
03 E-05
07 E-06
14 E-07
24 E-08
35 E-09
45 E-10
52 E-11
56 E-12
58 E-13
59 E-14
59 E-15
59 E-16

8
9
10
11
12

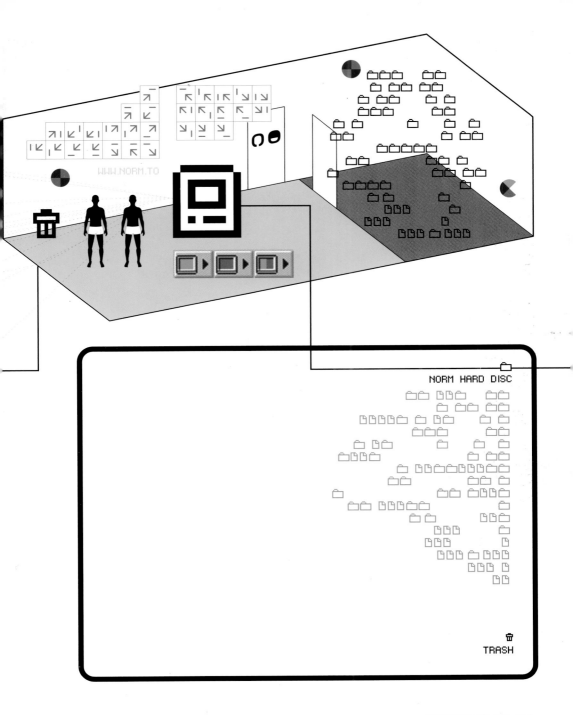

NORM HARD DISC

TRASH

```
☐ NORM HARD DISK ▣▤        ☐ NORM HARD DISK ▣▤        ☐ NORM HARD DISK ▣▤
  ▷ 🗀 SYSTEM                ▷ 🗀 SYSTEM                ▷ 🗀 SYSTEM
  ▷ 🗀 SOFTWARE             ▽ 🗀 SOFTWARE             ▽ 🗀 SOFTWARE
  ▷ 🗀 TYPES                  ▷ 🗀 ILLUSTRATOR 8.0       ▷ 🗀 ILLUSTRATOR 8.0
  ▷ 🗀 DOCUMENTS             ▷ 🗀 SUPER PAINT 2.0       ▷ 🗀 SUPER PAINT 2.0
                             ▷ 🗀 FONTOGRAPHER 4.1.5    ▷ 🗀 FONTOGRAPHER 4.1.5
                           ▽ 🗀 TYPES                 ▽ 🗀 TYPES
                             ▷ 🗀 NORM FONTS            ▽ 🗀 NORM FONTS
                             ▷ 🗀 REST OF THE WORLD FONTS  ▷ 🗀 ASFOUND
                           ▽ 🗀 DKS                      ▷ 🗀 BELINDA
                             ▷ 🗀 NORM DOCS              ▷ 🗀 ITALIA
                             ▷ 🗀 JOB DOCS               ▷ 🗀 MOLECULE
                                                        ▷ 🗀 NORMETICA
                                                        ▷ 🗀 PRIMARY
                                                        ▷ 🗀 PIXELSTYLE
                                                        ▷ 🗀 SIMILAR
                                                        ▷ 🗀 SIMPLE
                                                        ▷ 🗀 SIMULATION
                                                        ▷ 🗀 STANDARD
                                                        ▷ 🗀 SUPERA
                                                        ▷ 🗀 TETRA
                                                        ▷ 🗀 OCTAGON
                                                        ▷ 🗀 CRUISER
                                                        ▷ 🗀 EMC
                                                        ▷ 🗀 HAMMER
                                                        ▷ 🗀 P22
                                                        ▷ 🗀 ODERMATT
                                                        ▷ 🗀 MAXI
                                                        ▷ 🗀 REGULAR
                                                        ▷ 🗀 SCRABBLE
                                                        ▷ 🗀 SEEBAD
                                                        ▷ 🗀 SHAHRZAD
                                                        ▷ 🗀 ZENTRAL
                                                      ▽ 🗀 REST OF THE WORLD FONTS
                                                        ▷ 🗀 HELVETICA NEUE
                                                    ▽ 🗀 DKS
                                                      ▽ 🗀 NORM DOKS
                                                        ▷ 🗀 INTRODUCTION
                                                        ▷ 🗀 INTRODUCTIONWEB
                                                        ▷ 🗀 THINGS
                                                        ▷ 🗀 THINGSWEB
                                                        ▷ 🗀 SHAHRZAD
                                                      ▽ 🗀 JOB DOKS
                                                        ▷ 🗀 MOSTBEAUTIFUL.1
                                                        ▷ 🗀 ENJOY/SURVIVE
                                                        ▷ 🗀 MFG
                                                        ▷ 🗀 PHYS. ARCHITECTUR
                                                        ▷ 🗀 HGKZ
                                                        ▷ 🗀 MIUZE
                                                        ▷ 🗀 P22
                                                        ▷ 🗀 XXX
```

□ NORM HARD DISK 回日
L=2
▷ 🗀 SYSTEM
▽ 🗀 SOFTWARE
  ▷ 🗀 ILLUSTRATOR 8.0
  ▷ 🗀 SUPER PAINT 2.0
  ▷ 🗀 FONTOGRAPHER 4.1.5
▽ 🗀 TYPES
  ▽ 🗀 NORM FONTS
    ▷ 🗀 ASFOUND
    ▷ 🗀 BELINDA
    ▽ 🗀 COMFORT
      ▷ 🗎 C_MEDIUM
      ▷ 🗎 C_BOLD
    ▷ 🗀 ITALIA
    ▷ 🗀 MOLECULE
    ▽ 🗀 NORMETICA
      ▷ 🗎 N_A
      ▷ 🗎 N_A_EXPERT
      ▷ 🗎 N_B
      ▷ 🗎 N_B_EXPERT
      ▷ 🗎 N_C
      ▷ 🗎 N_EXPERT
    ▷ 🗀 PRIMARY
    ▷ 🗀 PIXELSTYLE
    ▽ 🗀 PRIMA
      ▷ 🗎 P_1
      ▷ 🗎 P_2
      ▷ 🗎 P_3
      ▷ 🗎 P_NORMAL
      ▷ 🗎 P_DICK
      ▷ 🗎 P_VOLLFETT
    ▽ 🗀 SIMILAR
      ▷ 🗎 S_MEDIUM
      ▷ 🗎 S_ULTRA
    ▽ 🗀 SIMPLE
      ▷ 🗎 S_LIGHT
      ▷ 🗎 S_LIGHT_EXPERT
      ▷ 🗎 S_LIGHT_OBLIQUE
      ▷ 🗎 S_EXPERT
      ▷ 🗎 S_REGULAR
      ▷ 🗎 S_TITLING
      ▷ 🗎 S_REGULAR_OBLIQUE
      ▷ 🗎 S_BOLD
      ▷ 🗎 S_BOLD_OBLIQUE_TITLING
      ▷ 🗎 S_BOLD_TITLING
    ▽ 🗀 SIMULATION
      ▷ 🗎 S_MEDIUM
      ▷ 🗎 S_ULTRA
    ▷ 🗀 STANDARD
    ▷ 🗀 SUPERA
      ▷ 🗎 S_LIGHT
      ▷ 🗎 S_BOLD
    ▽ 🗀 TETRA
      ▷ 🗎 T_A
      ▷ 🗎 T_B
    ▷ 🗀 OCTAGON
    ▷ ▷ ▷ 🗎 FREE DOWNLOAD ▷ WWW.NORM.TO
    ▷ 🗀 CRUISER
    ▷ 🗀 EMC

▽ 🗀 HAMMER
  ▷ 🗎 HAMMER REGULAR
▷ 🗀 P22
▷ 🗀 ODERMATT
▷ 🗀 MAXI
▷ 🗀 REGULAR [1]
  ▷ 🗎 R_REGULAR
  ▷ 🗎 R_BOLD
  ▷ 🗎 R_EXTENDED
▷ 🗀 SCRABBLE
▽ 🗀 SEEBAD
  ▷ 🗎 S_POSITIV
  ▷ 🗎 S_NEGATIV
▷ 🗀 SHAHRZAD
▷ 🗀 ZENTRAL
▽ 🗀 REST OF THE WORLD FONTS
  ▷ 🗀 HELVETICA NEUE
▽ 🗀 DKS
  ▽ 🗀 NORM DOKS
    ▷ 🗀 INTRODUCTION
    ▷ 🗀 INTRODUCTIONWEB
    ▷ 🗀 THINGS
    ▷ 🗀 THINGSWEB
    ▷ 🗀 SHAHRZAD
  ▽ 🗀 JOB DOKS
    ▷ 🗀 MOSTBEAUTIFUL.1
    ▷ 🗀 ENJOY/SURVIVE
    ▷ 🗀 MFG
    ▷ 🗀 PHYS. ARCHITECTUR
    ▷ 🗀 HGKZ
    ▷ 🗀 MIUZE
    ▷ 🗀 P22
    ▷ 🗀 XXX

🗑 ▽ 🗀 TRASH
  ▷ 🗀 QXP
  ▷ 🗀 AD
  ▽ 🗀 [1]
    ▽ 🗎
      FUCK YOU CHRIS REHBERGER_FUCK,
      AND YOU ROTTEN MONI_INOM BITCH.
      BURN IN 🔥 [ WE DID IT FIRST ].

**E**lectric **E**yes **A**re **E**verywhere

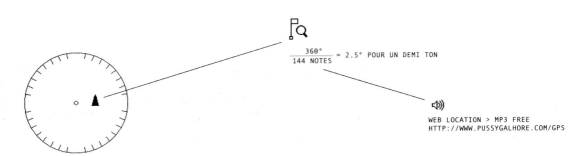

$$\frac{360°}{144 \text{ NOTES}} = 2.5° \text{ POUR UN DEMI TON}$$

WEB LOCATION > MP3 FREE
HTTP://WWW.PUSSYGALHORE.COM/GPS

GPS AMBIENT-MIX
- - - - - - - - - - - - - - - - - - - - - - - - - -
GPS LOCATION
N                           46°28.858
E                           006°46.155
LOC SUI                     548530
                            147819
ALTITUDE                    556 M.
HEURES                      11H35 AM
- - - - - - - - - - - - - - - - - - - - - - - - - -
ADRESSE                     CHEMIN DU MUR BLANC
                            1812 RIVAZ / VD
                            SWITZERLAND

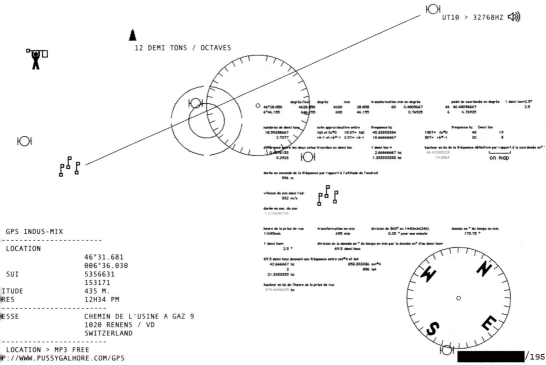

UT10 > 32768HZ

12 DEMI TONS / OCTAVES

GPS INDUS-MIX
------------------------
LOCATION
                46°31.681
                006°36.030
SUI             5356631
                153171
ITUDE           435 M.
RES             12H34 PM
------------------------
ESSE            CHEMIN DE L'USINE A GAZ 9
                1020 RENENS / VD
                SWITZERLAND
------------------------
LOCATION > MP3 FREE
P://WWW.PUSSYGALHORE.COM/GPS

/195

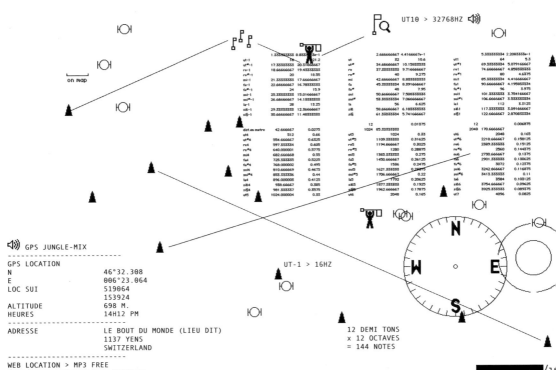

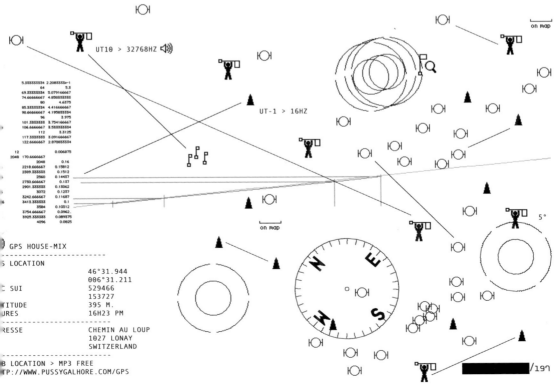

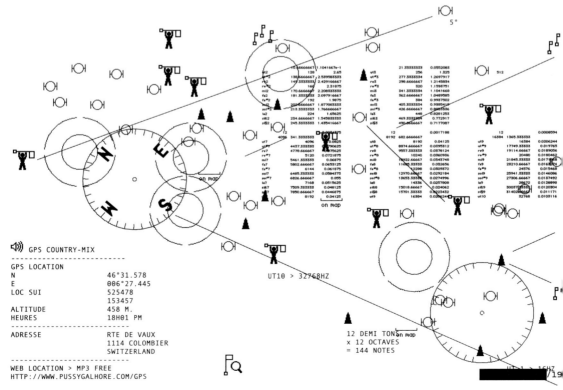

| ut5 | 21.33333333 | 0.0552083 |
| ut2 | 128 | 2.65 | ut*5 | 256 | 1.325 |
| ut*2 | 138.6666667 | 2.539583333 | re5 | 277.3333334 | 1.2697917 |
| re2 | 149.3333333 | 2.429166667 | re*5 | 296.6666667 | 1.21458334 |
| re*2 | 160 | 2.31875 | mi5 | 320 | 1.1395751 |
| mi2 | 170.6666667 | 2.20791667 | fa5 | 341.3333334 | 1.1041668 |
| fa2 | 181.3333333 | 2.09791667 | fa*5 | 362.6666667 | 1.0489585 |
| fa*2 | 192 | 1.9875 | sol5 | 384 | 0.9987502 |
| sol2 | 202.6666667 | 1.87708333 | sol*5 | 405.3333334 | 0.950541 |
| sol*2 | 213.3333333 | 1.766666667 | la5 | 426.6666667 | 0.895536 |
| la2 | 224 | 1.65625 | la#5 | 448 | 0.8281253 |
| si#2 | 234.6666667 | 1.545833333 | si#5 | 469.3333334 | 0.772917 |
| si#2 | 245.3333333 | 1.435416667 | si#5 | 490.6666667 | 0.7177087 |
| | | | 12 | | 0.0017198 | | | | 12 | | |
| ut7 | 4096 | | ut8 | 8192 | 0.04125 | ut9 | 16384 | 0.0206244 |
| ut*7 | 4096 | 0.0825 | ut*8 | 8974.666667 | 0.0395312 | ut*9 | 17749.33333 | 0.019765 |
| re7 | 4437.333333 | 0.079025 | re8 | 9557.333333 | 0.0378124 | re9 | 19114.66667 | 0.0189054 |
| re*7 | 4778.666667 | 0.075625 | re*8 | 10240 | 0.0360936 | re*9 | 20480 | 0.0180462 |
| mi7 | 5120 | 0.0721875 | mi8 | 10922.66667 | 0.0343740 | mi9 | 21845.33333 | 0.0171868 |
| fa7 | 5461.333333 | 0.06875 | fa8 | 11605.33333 | 0.032656 | fa9 | 28210.66667 | 0.0163280 |
| fa*7 | 5802.666667 | 0.0653125 | fa*8 | 12288 | 0.0309372 | fa*9 | 24576 | 0.0154688 |
| sol7 | 6485.333333 | 0.0594375 | sol8 | 12970.66667 | 0.0292184 | sol9 | 25941.33333 | 0.0146086 |
| sol*7 | 6826.666667 | 0.055 | sol*8 | 13653.33333 | 0.0274996 | sol*9 | 27306.66667 | 0.0137492 |
| la7 | 7168 | 0.0515625 | la8 | 14336 | 0.0257808 | la9 | 28672 | 0.0128898 |
| si#7 | 7509.333333 | 0.046125 | si#8 | 15018.66667 | 0.0240462 | si#9 | 30007 | 0.0120304 |
| si#7 | 7850.666667 | 0.0446875 | si#8 | 15701.33333 | 0.0223432 | si#9 | 31402 | 0.0111171 |
| | 8192 | 0.04125 | ut9 | 16384 | 0.0206244 | ut10 | 32768 | 0.0103116 |

5°

on map

UT10 > 32768HZ

12 DEMI TON
× 12 OCTAVES
= 144 NOTES

GPS COUNTRY-MIX
------------------------------
GPS LOCATION
N              46°31.578
E              006°27.445
LOC SUI        525478
               153457
ALTITUDE       458 M.
HEURES         18H01 PM
------------------------------
ADRESSE        RTE DE VAUX
               1114 COLOMBIER
               SWITZERLAND
------------------------------
WEB LOCATION > MP3 FREE
HTTP://WWW.PUSSYGALHORE.COM/GPS

raar////judo

# Appenzell

SWITZERLAND

UNIQUELY SPICY

Fromage Käse Fo...

Appenzel...

®

Since 1886, there has been a weather-station master at the summit of the mountain- who telegraph his daily measurement to the cities of Europe. In the autumn of 97, a lonely couple inhabit the lonely station. A former Austrian officer feel he had been cheated. He decided to prove the worth that- by being the first to climb up to the summit in winter- the post of stationmaster should have been given to him. Once up there- in the station covered with ice- up in the sky- the life and death struggle begins. All three are stuck at the summit and there is only enough food for two of them.

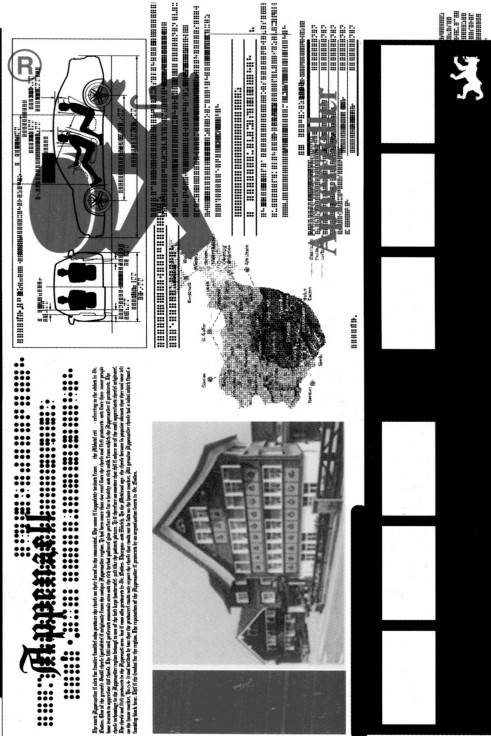

# Appenzell

## Appenzeller

The name Appenzeller & asks for smaller familiar value produces the cheese we have found in the mountains...

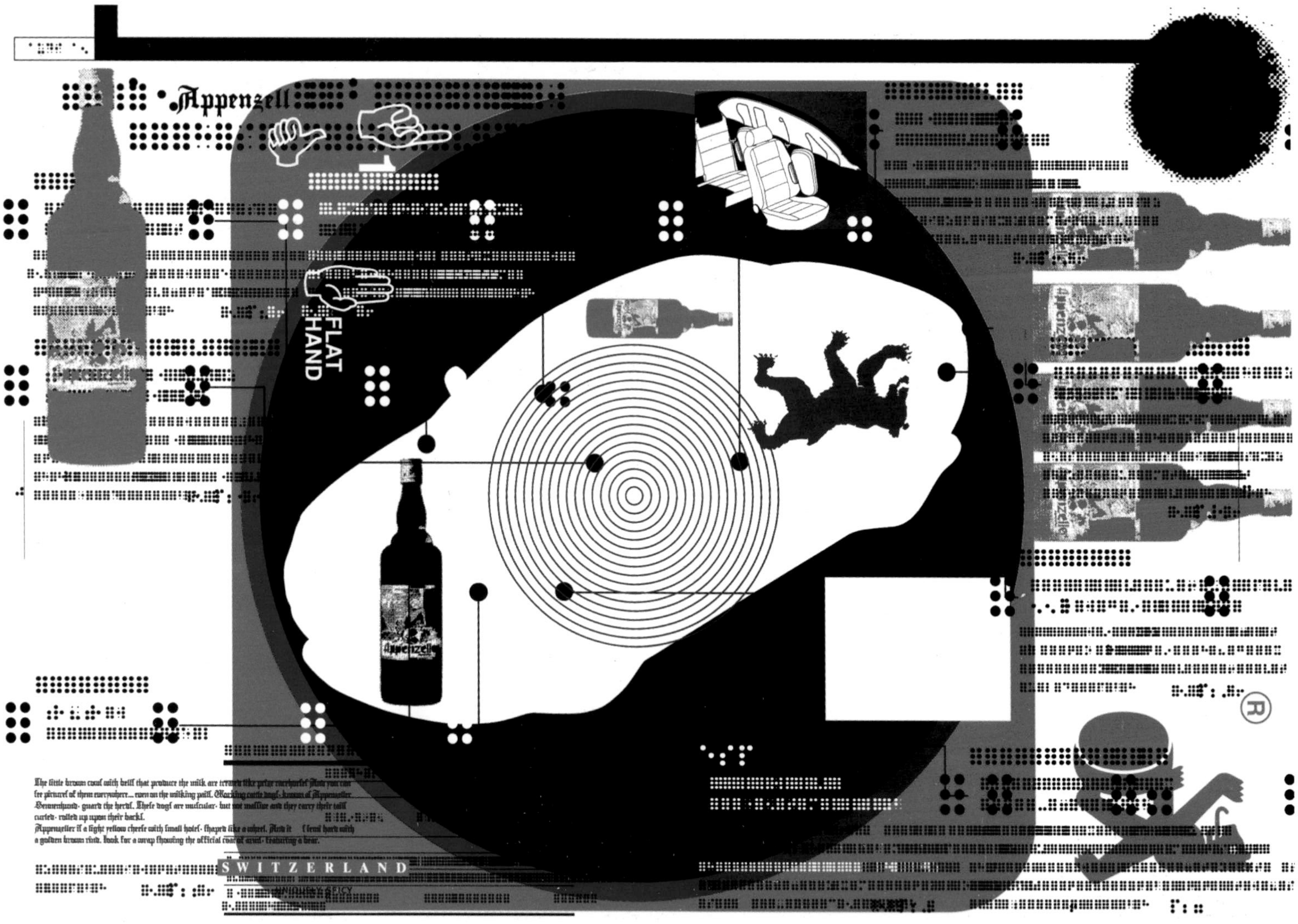

FLAT
HAND

1

Appenzell

*Appenzeller*

SWITZERLAND

®

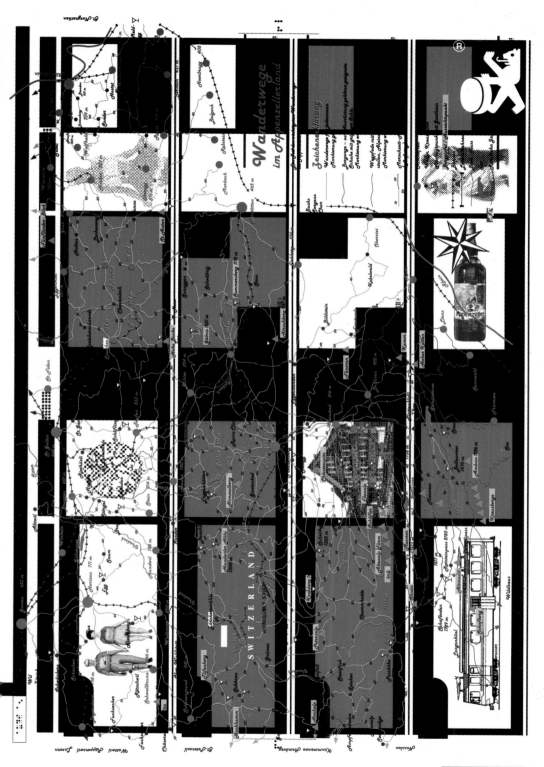

switzerland/doesn't/exist//it/is/an/invention/of/the/swiss/graphic/designers////we/didn't/know/this//
however/one/just/has/to/look/a/little/closer/at/its/geography////we/soon/realize/that/the/work/has/been/
well/finished//conscientiously//neatly//nothing/sticks/out/or/overlaps/the/margins////vast/horizons/of/
pure/fresh/air/and/clichés//large/spaces/very/much/like/the/21/inch/screens/of/their/conceivors////
first/of/all/a/country/that/would/have/the/exact/outline/of/the/swiss/map//a/country/where/a/single/
typeface/helvetica/?/univers/?/would/allow/three/different/written/languages////a/culinary/heritage/as/
well//it/is/the/swiss/cheese/that/gave/the/circle/its/shape////from/a/portion/was/born/the/triangle/and/
a/piece/of/chocolate/became/the/origin/of/the/square////from/this/controlled/simplicity/was/born/all/the/
scenery/that/the/swiss/have/always/taken/so/much/pride/in////a/few/full/colours/for/the/lakes////as/for/
the/mountain/pastures/a/hideous/green//impossible/to/coordinate/with/the/red/of/the/national/flag/and/its/
little//neatly/centred/cross////for/the/rest/nothing/really/straight//vectorial/slopes/whose/summits/
have/been/left/white//surely/from/a/lack/of/time/or/inspiration//on/the/facade/the/mountaineers/find/
without/difficulty/the/anchorage/points//essential/pathfinders/on/which/to/lean/on/to/accomplish/their/
ascent////from/above/they/will/be/able/to/distinguish/quite/clearly/the/colour/chart/of/the/countryside/
the/parametered/tracings/of/the/rivers/and/roads/drawn/by/m/bézier////the/scrupulous/compositions/of/the/
forests/leaves/us/thoughtful////under/the/shade/of/a/bold/italic/and/mossy/oak/tree//grow/young/trees/
ultralight/but/strong/and/straight////occasionally/a/pointer/crosses/the/pantone/279/c/sky////having/
admired/his/rgb/reflection/in/an/elliptical/puddle//he/flies/over/the/laboured/fields/where/farmers/
outline/a/complex/base-grid/that/extends/itself/to/the/pixel/paved/paths/of/a/nearby/village////justified/
to/the/left//chalets/succeed/one/another////in/front/of/each/are/well/centred/small//neatly/kept/
gardens/surrounded/by/a/0.3/point/line////these/constructions/owe/more/to/formel/rigour/that/presides/
over/their/assembling/than/to/the/wooden/logs/that/actually/compose/them////the/workshop/of/the/day/comes/
to/an/end/and/the/layers/have/been/flattened////savouring/a/juicy/well/earned/apple/s//the/men/return/to/
their/homes////waiting/for/their/arrival//their/wives/muse//listening/to/an/old/jaz/…

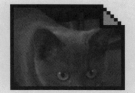

name/design/company///////diy/////rue/de/genève/19/1003/lausanne/vd/switzerland
cuendet/philippe////jaccottet/laurence////liechti/ivan

034////book/cover//septembre//nicolas/pages//flammarion//2002
035////illustrations//septembre//nicolas/pages//flammarion//2002
036////collection/+41//2002
037////collection/+41//2002
038////skate//gp2002//2002
039////some/ //diy/fonts//2002

138////plage/de/rivaz/1812/rivaz/vd
139////plage/de/rivaz/1812/rivaz/vd


places/to/be////
////auberge/de/dully//1195/dully/vd
////domobile//chemin/de/la/girarde/1s/1066/épalinges/vd
////242/shop//rue/des/côtes-de-montbenon/s/1003/lausanne/vd
////place/de/pique-nique//route/chexbres-chardonne/1803/chardonne/vd
////lac/retaud/1865/les/diablerets/vd

name/design/company////`a---b`////rue/des/côtes-de-montbenon/6/1003/lausanne/vd/switzerland
benedetto/angelo

040////poster//lazy/designer/tool/application//1999
lazy/designer/tool/contains/samples/from/angelo/benedetto's/écal/diploma/which/consists/of/a/number/of/
interactive/works////you/can/experience/each/work/by/clicking/at/intervals////lazy/designer/tool/has/been/
awarded/the/swiss/design/prize/2001
041////strada/typeface//2002
font/inspired/by/swiss/road/markings

140////incognito/enzo's/barbhair/shop//rue/des/côtes-de-montbenon/5/1003/lausanne/vd
141////incognito/enzo's/barbhair/shop//rue/des/côtes-de-montbenon/5/1003/lausanne/vd
enzo's/barbhair/shop/is/located/in/le/flon/lausanne////enzo/is/a/vinyl/junkie/and/spends/a/lot/of/time/in/
record/fairs/to/find/some/rare/grooves/for/his/collections////so/go/to/enzo's/barbhair/shop/for/a/haircut/
and/music/conversation


places/to/be////
////242/shop//rue/des/côtes-de-montbenon/5/1003/lausanne/vd
////16/tons//anwandstrasse/25/8004/zürich/zh
////mono/records//froschaugasse/8/8001/zürich/zh
////oldie's/shop//bollwerk/19/3011/bern/be
////raspect/reggae/and/juice//boulevard/james-fazy/4/1201/genève/ge

name/design/company////and-or////clergère/9/1800/vevey/vd/switzerland
bettler/aalex

142////avenue/de/cour/4/lausanne/vd////chemin/de/la/ficelle/lausanne/vd
143////avenue/de/la/harpe/rue/jean-jacques-cart/lausanne/vd////avenue/edouard/dapples/lausanne/vd////
parking/de/bellerive/avenue/de/rhodanie/lausanne/vd


places/to/be////
////quai/maria/belgia/1800/vevey/vd
////théâtre/sévelin/36/1004/lausanne/vd
////usine/de/production/d'eau/potable//marquisat/2/1025/st-sulpice/vd
////service/des/eaux/de/villette//lavaux/1096/villette/vd

name/design/company////`aubry/bastien`////pfingstweidstrasse/31b/8005/zürich/zh/switzerland
aubry/bastien

042////poster//rote/fabrik//music/style/rock
043////flyer//bar/in/the/garage//music/style/80's/synthesizer/sound////flyer//rote/fabrik//music/style/
mambo-kraftwerk////illustration//play/it/rough/2//airdog/recording////invitation//migros/museum////flyer//
rote/fabrik//music/style/abstract/rock////illustration//play/it/rough/2//airdog/recording
044////back/cover//play/it/rough/2//airdog/recording//music/style/elektrofunk/drum/and/bass
045////cover//play/it/rough/2//airdog/recording//music/style/elektrofunk/drum/and/bass
046////cover//schwule/mädschen//fettes/brot//yo/mama/recording//music/style/hip/hop
047////cover//demo/tape//fettes/brot//yo/mama/recording//music/style/hip/hop

144////garage/ankerstrasse/8004/zürich/zh
145////garage/ankerstrasse/8004/zürich/zh
146////garage/ankerstrasse/8004/zürich/zh
147////garage/ankerstrasse/8004/zürich/zh
148////garage/ankerstrasse/8004/zürich/zh
149////garage/ankerstrasse/8004/zürich/zh
special/dank/to/the/bar/team/and/michela/montalbetti/for/the/superheld/picture////special/fuck/to/the/
promoteur/immobilier


places/to/be////
////le/peupequignot/ju
////la/bosse/ju
////le/creux/des/biches/ju
////la/seigne/aux/femmes/ju
////le/peuchapatte/ju

jura/power/!

name/design/company////born/julia////1e/constantijn/huygensstr./20/3/1054/bw/amsterdam/the/netherlands
born/julia

048////series/of/3/posters//program-folder//series/of/6/postcards//hoi/dancetheatre//piece/by/metzger//
zimmermann//de/perrot//2001////poster/vedute/reeks//vedute/foundation//2000//collaboration/with/daria/
holme/under/dj////calendar//2001/2002//calff/and/meischke//2001//collaboration/with/daria/holme/under/
dj////poster/with/eyelets//abc/sections//2000
049////series/of/3/posters//program-folder//series/of/6/postcards//hoi/dancetheatre//piece/by/metzger//
zimmermann//de/perrot//2001////poster/vedute/reeks//vedute/foundation//2000//collaboration/with/daria/
holme/under/dj////calendar//2001/2002//calff/and/meischke//2001//collaboration/with/daria/holme/under/
dj////poster/with/eyelets//abc/sections//2000
050////various/invitations/for/exhibitions//folders//posters//booklets//leaflets//envelope//gallery/w139/
amsterdam//2001/2002//collaboration/with/daria/holme/under/dj////folded/map//swiss/design/studios//swiss/
federal/office/of/culture//design/service//2001////program-newspaper//folder//posters//alicia/framis//
loneliness/in/the/city/remix/buildings//migros/museum//2000//collaboration/with/elektrosmog////book/
schrift//2000////notepad//2000
051////various/invitations/for/exhibitions//folders//posters//booklets//leaflets//envelope//gallery/w139/
amsterdam//2001/2002//collaboration/with/daria/holme/under/dj////folded/map//swiss/design/studios//swiss/
federal/office/of/culture//design/service//2001////program-newspaper//folder//posters//alicia/framis//
loneliness/in/the/city/remix/buildings//migros/museum//2000//collaboration/with/elektrosmog////book/
schrift//2000////notepad//2000

150////rifugio/garzonera//piotta/quinto/ti
151////rifugio/garzonera//piotta/quinto/ti
152////rifugio/garzonera//piotta/quinto/ti
153////rifugio/garzonera//piotta/quinto/ti


places/to/be////
////helen/faigle//neumarkt/7/8001/zürich/zh
most/beautiful/grocery-shop/!
////müdespacher//marktgasse/11/8001/zürich/zh
best/cheese/!
////bürli/vorderer/sternen/at/bellevue
best/bratwurst/!
////new/point//langstrasse
best/poulet-kebab/!

name/design/company////`cottenceau/geoffrey`////rue/du/maupas/22/1004/lausanne/vd/switzerland
cottenceau/geoffrey

ms2////caribou//sample/from/geoffrey/cottenceau´s/écal/diploma//2001
ms3////éléphant//sample/from/geoffrey/cottenceau´s/écal/diploma//2001

.ss////jet/d´eau/de/genève//jetée/des/eaux-vives/genève/ge
collaboration/with/gaillardot/julien


places/to/be////
"///musée/d´histoire/naturelle//route/de/malagnou/genève/ge
"///fulguro.//avenue/du/temple/s/1020/renens/vd
"///pmu/de/carouge//genève/ge
"///creu/du/van/ne
"///café/de/l´univers//place/du/coq/d´inde/ne

name/design/company////`electronic/curry/ltd`////rue/des/vieux-grenadiers/10/1205/genève/ge/switzerland
bili/christian

054////illustrations//santis/republic//2002
055////self/promotion/stickers//place/photo/here//2001
056////pamphlet//no/more/pipeline//2001
057////flyers//see/sex/and/son//2000


156////quartier/des/banques//rive/gauche/genève/ge
157////quartier/des/banques//rive/gauche/genève/ge
158////quartier/des/banques//rive/gauche/genève/ge
159////quartier/des/banques//rive/gauche/genève/ge
collaboration/with/schönwehrs


places/to/be////
////flea/market//genève/ge
////le/thé//rue/des/bains/6s/genève/ge
////falafels//rue/des/eaux-vives/genève/ge
facing/the/cinema/les/scalas
////flea/market//zürich/zh
////hiltl//sihlstrasse/zürich/zh

ame/design/company////`Fehr/hansjakob`////danziger/strasse/51/10435/berlin/germany
ehr/hansjakob

60////rue/william/haldimand/lausanne/vd
61////rue/william/haldimand/lausanne/vd
62////rue/william/haldimand/lausanne/vd
63////rue/william/haldimand/lausanne/vd
potfinder/indoor////1////set/up/the/basic-module/with/the/two/outdoor-modules////simply/attach////
he/monitor/consists/of/a/2.3″/tft/display////the/sensor-modul/consists/of/an/electronic/compass/and/an/
nclinometer////the/information/of/the/sensors/are/analysed/by/the/computer/and/move/a/panoramic/picture/
n/the/monitor////like/this/the/impression/of/a/virtual/world/occurs////2////connect/the/spotfinder/to/
he/usb/port/of/your/computer////3////switch/on/your/computer////4////load/the/spotfinder´s/programme/
rom/the/floppy/disk////5////choose/a/place/in/the/place-list/of/the/programme////6////hold/the/
potfinder/in/front/of/your/eye/and/stand/in/the/centre/of/the/room////7////navigate/virtually/through/
he/room/by/simply/moving/your/head////you/will/easily/find/the/most/beautiful/view/of/the/place////
lease/follow/our/instructions////we/have/already/found/the/most/beautiful/outlooks/for/you////this/way/
ou/are/better/prepared/for/your/coming/journey/and/know/already/all/well/worth/seeing/points
potfinder/outdoor////1////modify/the/spotfinder´s/basic-module/with/the/compass/angle/adapter////in/an/
nknown/place/you/will/be/overwhelmed/by/all/the/different/impressions////it/will/be/difficult/to/find/
he/best/views////luckily/you/have/practised/peacefully/at/home/and/have/noticed/the/coordinates/of/one/
r/another/outlook////otherwise/check/the/proposed/coordinates////2////take/the/spotfinder/outdoor/put/
t/in/front/of/your/eye////the/compass/and/the/goniometer/are/mirrored/directly/into/the/pipe/by/an/
crylic/glass/reflector////3////spin/on/yourself/until/the/wanted/coordinates/are/displayed////4////
over/the/light/opening/of/the/compass/angle-module/with/your/hand/and/break/off/the/data/reflection/
/5////you/will/see/the/wanted/outlook


laces/to/be////
///african/restaurant//red/sea//rue/de/la/tour/17/1004/lausanne/vd
at/with/fingers
///main/station//platform/24//zürich/zh
alk/on/the/platform/from/one/stair/to/the/other/and/take/a/look/at/the/watch
///station//lausanne/vd
ook/around/and/find/the/different/types/on/the/lausanne/plaques
///station//brunau/allmend/II
alk/in/direction/of/wolishofen/beside/the/river/to/the/sihl/kiosk////eat/a/hot/dog/!
arning/there/are/always/many/dogs/around/!
///restaurant//la/vache/qui/vole//place/centale/2b/1920/martigny/vs
ine/wine/bar/restaurant

name/design/company////Fulguro/////avenue/du/temple/s/1020/renens/vd/switzerland
decroux/cédric////fidalgo/yves////jaccard/axel


058////euro/belts//prototypes//colour/ribbons//nylon/straps//engraved/metal/buckles//écal's/exhibition/
le/botte-cul//2002
059////lamps//prototypes//screen/printed/polycarbonate/sheets//2002
pick/up/the/design/you/like/and/build/it/yourself/!


164////avenue/du/léman/1020/renens/vd
165////e62/direction/genève/1260/nyon/vd
166////zone/industrielle/de/l'île/falcon/3960/sierre/vs
167////chemin/des/condémines/1904/vernayaz/vs
paper/invasion/on/swiss/landscapes


places/to/be////
////café/de/la/gare//bulle/fr
super/fondue/restaurant
////vidy/lausanne/vd
under/the/big/tree
////skilift//le/chalet-à-gobet/vd
////parc/des/eaux-vives/genève/ge
////ruine/du/vieux/château//saint-cergue/vd

ame/design/company////gtv////chemin/de/la/cocarde/10/1024/écublens/vd/switzerland
urin/gilles////turin/vincent

60////superpersonnages//sample/from/gtv´s/écal/diploma//2000
61////poster//get/angry//perspectives/romandes/3//musée/cantonal/des/beaux-arts/lausanne//écal//2001
62////catalogue//bcu-art/acquisition/91-01//écal//2001
63////poster//université/populaire/de/lausanne//2001
64////poster/project//expo.02//2002
65////gtvphantom//gtv´s/email/signature//2002

68////forêt/route/de/la/salle-des-fayards/vernand-dessus/le/mont-sur-lausanne/vd
69////forêt/route/de/la/salle-des-fayards/vernand-dessus/le/mont-sur-lausanne/vd
ample/from/gtv´s/écal/postgraduate/diploma//2002

laces/to/be////
///boucherie/jean-louis/bolay//route/de/cottens/1141/sévery/vd
he/best/barbecue/meat/!
///uchitomi//traiteur/épicerie/japonais//rue/de/zürich/45/1201/genève/ge
he/best/sushis/in/switzerland/!
///le/nouveau/surplus//route/de/chavornay/1350/orbe/vd
or/helicopter/turbines/and/letter/stencils
///cantine/de/la/chocolatière//route/de/la/chocolatière/6/1026/échandens/vd
wooden/shed/a/300g/steak/served/on/slate/french/fries/and/vegetables
///piscine/de/bellevaux//route/du/pavement/1018/lausanne/vd
/pool/in/the/middle/of/a/forest

name/design/company////`güdel/benjamin`////schöneggstrasse/s/8004/zürich/zh/switzerland
güdel/benjamin

066////t-shirt/artwork//jesus//harper-design//1997
067////self/promotion/illustration//quang//1999
068////illustration//eat/this/bitch/!//die/weltwoche//2002
069////illustration//eat/this/bitch/!//die/weltwoche//2002
070////illustration//demo//soda/magazine//2001
071////illustration//demo//soda/magazine//2001

places/to/be////
////total/bar//tellstrasse/20/zürich/zh
my/favourite/bar/!
////beige//josefstrasse/10/12/zürich/zh
young/hip/swiss/styling/mode////they/show/their/own/label
////il/pentagramma//just/next/to/beige
best/biggest/warm/italian/sandwiches/in/town/!
////flea/market//petersplatz/basel/bs
beautiful/atmosphere/every/saturday
////from/belluue/to/zürihorn//all/along/the/lake
make/a/walk/on/a/sunny/weekend////crowded/with/secondos/bongos/!/and/all/that/easy/going/!

ame/design/company////`happypets`////avenue/du/tribunal-fédéral/3/1005/lausanne/vd/switzerland
ont/violène////monnier/patrick////henny/cédric

n2////poster//tools/on/the/loose//happypets//workshop//2002
n3////wallpaper//t-shirts//stickers//brochures//postcards//posters//label/usine//2002
n4////illustration//revival//the/face/magazine//2002
n5////illustration//creative//the/face/magazine//2002
n6////poster//chantecler/la/belle/de/nuit//documentary/film//2002
n7////stickers//brochures//postcards//posters//visual/identity//fabriclch//2001

n0////forêt/1084/carrouge/vd
n1////forêt/1084/carrouge/vd
n2////route/du/borgeau/1084/carrouge/vd
n3////route/du/borgeau/1084/carrouge/vd
n4////le/carrouge/route/du/borgeau/1084/carrouge/vd
n5////le/carrouge/route/du/borgeau/1084/carrouge/vd


laces/to/be////
///captain/cook/pub//rue/enning/2/1003/lausanne/vd
or/getting/wasted/!
///quai/des/brunes//avenue/du/tribunal-fédéral/1/1005/lausanne/vd
ood/lunch/menu/!
///zinéma//rue/du/maupas/4/1000/lausanne/vd
mall/independent/cinema
///l'elac//rue/de/genève/19/1003/lausanne/vd
ontemporary/art
///paradoxe/perdu//place/grenus/3/1201/ge
ots/of/gadgets/!

name/design/company////`kappeler/marc////brunner/bianca////moiré`////hardturmstrasse/102/8005/zürich/zh/
switzerland
kappeler/marc////brunner/bianca

078////birdposter//silkscreen/on/standard/sticker-sheet//wuhrplatzfest//2001
079////birdposter//silkscreen/on/standard/sticker-sheet//wuhrplatzfest//2001
080////barkposter//silkscreen/on/color/paper//poster-action//2002
081////barkposter//silkscreen/on/color/paper//poster-action//2002

176////aarwilweg/3074/muri/bei/bern/be
177////aarwilweg/3074/muri/bei/bern/be
collaboration/with/greber/andreas

places/to/be////
////flussbad/unterer/letten//wasserwerkstrasse/141/8005/zürich/zh
////tea-room//gasometerstrasse/s/8005/zürich/zh
////sphères/bar/und/buch//hardturmstrasse/66/8005/zürich/zh
////dachstock/reitschule//neubrückstrasse/8/3012/bern/be
////aarebad/muri//3074/muri/bei/bern/be

ame/design/company////[la3l]////chemin/du/trabandan/s1/1006/lausanne/vd/switzerland
ousset/romain

e2////logo//cheval/de/bois//the/field//2002
e3////black/kine//sample/from/romain/rousset's/écal/diploma//2001
hanks/to/jon/werner/schmidt
e4////illustration//purple//2002
es////illustration//free/tibet//l'écal/au/centre/culturel/suisse/de/paris//2002

ne////rue/du/petit/chêne/lausanne/vd
ng////rue/du/petit/chêne/lausanne/vd
e/soulier/ailé////collaboration/with/gaillardot/julien//cottenceau/geoffrey


laces/to/be////
///zoo/de/servion//le/pralet/1077/servion/vd
///zoo/bois/du/petit/château//rue/des/électrices/32/2300/la/chaux-de-fonds/ne
///playground/du/belvédère//chemin/des/croix-rouges/13/1003/lausanne/vd
///musée/d'histoire/naturelle//route/de/malagnou/1/1208/genève/ge
///snack/ouchy//quai/jean-pascal/delamuraz/lausanne/vd

name/design/company////**lehmann/aude**////zurlindenstrasse/22s/8003/zürich/zh/switzerland
lehmann/aude

086////fabrikzeitung/166//politik-minderheitenpolitik-postpolitik//auflage/s000//herausgeberin/igrf/und/
ag/fabrikzeitung//erscheint/monatlich//fabrikzeitung/rote/fabrik//seestrasse/39s/8038/zürich//tel/01/482
40/60//fax/01/482/92/10//faz@rotefabrik.ch//korrektorat/stefan/bührer//andrea/leuthold//belichtung/
salinger/satz/ag/zürich//druck/ropress/zürich//inserateannahmeschluss/1s./des/vormonats//abopreis/
jährlich//inland/fr/30.-//ausland/fr/40.-//redaktion/übersetzung/tan/wälchli//gestaltung/manuel/krebs/norm
/aude/lehmann//die/schemen/beziehen/sich/auf/wandtaffelskizzen/die/ernesto/laclau/während/des/seminars/
gezeichnet/hat////silex/nr/1s//le/rapport/annuel//mai/00////silex/my/way//printed/by/medialis/offset/
berlin//edited/by/r/klanten//m/mischler//created/by/silex//die/deutsche/bibliothek//cip//einheitsaufnahm
/ein/titelsatz/für/diese/publikation/ist/bei/der/deutschen/bibliothek/erhältlich//dgu/die/gestalten/
verlag/berlin//2001//isbn/3-931126-6s-x//for/your/local/dgu/distributor/please/check/www.die-gestalten.de
////fabrikzeitung/169//independent/women//redaktion/tan/wälchli//gestaltung/aude/lehmann////1-6//6/s/w/
siebdruckte/poster//s94/x/710/mm//gefaltet/gebunden//albisetti//lehmann//shahbazi//lithos/druck/atelier/
jaune/bern//1s0/ex//zürich//2001

087////detailsorge//studienbereich/visuelle/gestaltung//hochschule/für/gestaltung/und/kunst/zürich//
diplom/2001//herausgeber/studienbereich/visuelle/gestaltung//gestaltung/anna/albisetti/und/aude/lehmann/
korrektorat/andrea/leuthold//druck/inka/druck/zürich//auflage/400////programm//schauspielhaus/zürich//
drei/schwestern//herausgegeben/von/der/schauspielhaus/zürich/ag//zeltweg/s/8032/zürich//saison/2001/02//
künstlerische/direktion/christoph/marthaler//kaufmännische/direktion/marcel/müller//redaktion/andrea/
schwitter//stefanie/carp//konzeption/cornel/windlin//benjamin/sommerhalder//alex/trüb//gestaltung/alex/
trüb//zeichnungen/von/aude/lehmann//druck/zürichsee/druckereien/ag/8712/stäfa//auflage/s000/ex////der/
berg/gegenüber//2001//1/2/aude/lehmann//2/2/tan/wälchli//nieues/verlag/zürich//70/ex////fabrikzeitung/17
/0s.11.2000-1s.12.2000//redaktion/tan/wälchli//konzept/und/gestaltung/aude/lehmann//alex/trüb/und/tan/
wälchli//alle/bilder/aus/zürcher/tages-/und/wochenzeitung////saisonvorschau//schauspielhaus/zürich/02/03.
herausgegeben/von/der/schauspielhaus/zürich/ag//zeltweg/s/8032/zürich//künstlerische/direktion/christoph
marthaler//kaufmännische/direktion/marcel/müller//konzeption/alex/trüb/und/benjamin/sommerhalder//
redaktion/dramaturgie//texte/stefanie/carp//bruno/hitz//robert/koall//andrea/schwieter//stephan/wetzel//
redaktion/abonnement-teil/christoph/stuehn//anzeigen/kretz/ag/feldmeilen//gestaltung/alex/trüb/und/
benjamin/sommerhalder//zeichnungen/aude/lehmann/und/bastien/aubry//the/incredible/4xss/crew/!/big/up/!/
spezieller/dank/an/till/fiegenbaum//inga-a/hansen//ann/kolb//reinhard/werner//cornel/windlin/und/ziegler
pepier/ag/grellingen//druck/zürichsee/druckereien/ag/8712/stäfa//lithografie/zürichsee/druckereien/ag/
8712/stäfa//einband/buchbinderei/burkhardt/ag/mönchaltorf//umschlag/carpentier/ag/zürich//auflage/3s´000/
redaktionsschluss/29./april/2002//änderungen/vorbehalten////silex/nr/17//vogue/gedruckt/mit/urs/jost/
druckwerkstatt/olten//2s0/ex//august/2001

181////mer/de/glace
182////mer/de/glace
183////mer/de/glace
184////mer/de/glace
18s////mer/de/glace
text/tan/wälchli////correction/will/holder

places/to/be////
////chutes/du/rhin/schaffhouse/sh
////3920/zermatt/us
at/the/foot/of/the/matterhorn/1616/m/high
////jungfraujoch/alpes/bernoises/be
34s7/m/high
////7s00/st./moritz/haute-engadine/gr
18s6-34s7/m/high
////kappel-brücke/luzern/lu

name/design/company////`mentary.com`////stöberstrasse/36/4055/basel/bs/switzerland
chapuisat/gregory

ø88////street/poster//money/and/value//2001
collaboration/with/bouvard/harold
ø89////street/poster//the/yummy/yummyintestines//2002

▮

places/to/be////
////pipifax//ankerstrasse/20/zürich/zh
the/small/world/of/silkscreened/books
////duplex//rue/des/amis/9/genève/ge
independent/gallery
////gaya/bazar//spalenvorstadt/basel/bs
all/the/planet´s/natural/drugs
////cargo/bar//rhin/river//st.johanns/rheinweg/46/basel/bs
swim/through/basel/and/have/a/beer/at/your/arrival/at/the/cargo/bar
////expresso/bar//place/de/la/navigation/genève/ge
a/good/pizza/at/the/bar

name/design/company////norm/////pfingstweidstrasse/31b/8005/zürich/zh/switzerland
bruni/dimitri////krebs/manuel


090////book//introduction//1999
091////book//laborproben//hochschule/für/gestaltung/und/kunst/zürich//studienbereich/visuelle/gestaltung/
2000
092////book//enjoy/survive//olaf/nicolai//migros/museum/für/gegenwartskunst//die/gestalten/verlag//
berlin//2001
collaboration/with/nicolai/olaf
093////magazine//shahrzad/1//shahbazi//tehrani//zolghadr//2002
collaboration/with/shahbazi/shirana//zolghadr/tirdad
094////book//the/most/beautiful/swiss/books//swiss/federal/office/of/culture//2002
photography/truniger/isabel
095////book//the/things//2002


186////pfingstweidstrasse/31b/8005/zürich/zh
187////pfingstweidstrasse/31b/8005/zürich/zh
188////pfingstweidstrasse/31b/8005/zürich/zh
189////pfingstweidstrasse/31b/8005/zürich/zh
190////pfingstweidstrasse/31b/8005/zürich/zh
191////pfingstweidstrasse/31b/8005/zürich/zh


places/to/be////
////rue/dufour/124/2502/bienne/be
4th/floor/on/the/left
////faubourg/du/jura/13/2502/bienne/be
1st/floor/on/the/right/2nd/floor/on/the/left
////rue/de/berne/22/1201/genève/ge
3rd/floor/studio/36
////marienstrasse/21/8003/zürich/zh
5th/floor
////zelgstrasse/9/8003/zürich/zh
1st/floor/on/the/left

name/design/company////paulus/lauris////avenue/de/morges/36/1004/lausanne/vd/switzerland
paulus/lauris

096////cibachrome/print/on/aluminium//gregor//écal//2001
097////photography//dessine-moi/une/montre//vogue/france//2001
098////digital/print//no/title//2002
099////digital/print//no/title//2002
100////digital/print//no/title//2002
101////cibachrome/print/on/aluminium//philippe//écal//2001

192////forêt/de/brison/1822/chernex/montreux/vd
193////forêt/de/brison/1822/chernex/montreux/vd


places/to/be////
////7842/bergün/gr
////café/restaurant/belvédère//grand-rue/36/1700/fr
////zoo/de/bâle//binningerstrasse/40/4011/bs
////musée/de/l'habitat/rural//ballenberg/3855/brienz/be
////plage/de/rivaz/1812/rivaz/vd

name/music/company////`pussy/galhore`
henny/cédric////huser/charles

194////chemin/du/mur/blanc/1812/rivaz/vd
195////chemin/de/l'usine/à/gaz/1020/renens/vd
196////le/bout/du/monde/1137/yens/vd
197////chemin/au/loup/1027/lonay/vd
198////route/de/vaux/1114/colombier/vd
gps/project/////audio/compositions/constructed/on/the/basis/of/gps/data////download/the/tracks/on/
www.pussygalhore.com


places/to/be////
////chemin/des/oiseaux/1028/préverenges/vd
have/a/walk
////disc-à-brac//import-disc/rue/de/la/tour/14/1003/lausanne/vd
ask/for/téo/or/geneviève/for/alternative/rock/and/namskeio/for/minimal/electro
////abraxas/club//chemin/du/stand/s/1003/pully/vd
////schmidt/musique//rue/du/sablon/2s/1110 morges/vd
vintage/synthesizers/collectors/and/news/super/prices/!
////maharaja//avenue/de/france/2/1004/lausanne/vd
best/indian/food/take/away/in/lausanne

```
name/design/company////raar/////seebahnstrasse/127/8003/zürich/zh/switzerland
arnold/rahel

102////illustration//swiss/miniature//victionary//viction/design//2002
103////illustration//swiss/miniature//victionary//viction/design//2002

200////pilatus/grap/sogn/gion/graubünden/luzern/lu
201////rosengartenstrasse/zürich/zh
collaboration/with/judo



places/to/be////
////7500/st./moritz/gr
take/the/rhb/train/from/st./moritz/to/posciavo
////glacier/aletsch/us
////xenix//kanzleistrasse/56/8004/zürich/zh
have/a/beer/watch/a/movie/!
////flussbad/unterer/letten//wasserwerkstrasse/141/8005/zürich/zh
////migros/museum//limmatstrasse/270/8005/zürich/zh
```

name/design/company////`sonderegger/alex`////10-27-205/tateno-cho/nerima-ku/tokyo/177-0054
sonderegger/alex


104////poster//anti/terror/exibition//tra/co/ltd//niigata-city/japan//2001
105////dr/t-shirts//dynamite/rabbit//2002
collaboration/with/kobayashi/miki
106////dr/t-shirts//dynamite/rabbit//2002
collaboration/with/kobayashi/miki
107////night/life//direct/records//tokyo//2002


202////ai/ar
203////ai/ar
204////ai/ar
205////ai/ar


places/to/be////
////säntis//www.saentis-cam.cnlab.ch
////villa/malpensata//riva/caccia/s/6900/lugano/ti
museum/of/modern/art
////hotel/schweizerhof//luzern/schweizerhofquai/3/6004/luzern/lu
////sedel/club//ilm/sedel/postfach/6346/6000/luzern/6/lu
////2800/delémont/ju

name/design/company////woodtli/martin////schöneggstrasse/5/8004/zürich/zh/switzerland
woodtli/martin

108////flyer//floatingskills//stadtgalerie/bern//2001
109////flyer//alan/turing/und/die/chiffriermaschine/enigma//digital/brainstorming//migros-kulturprozent//
2002
110////flyer//oh/mein/papa//stadtgalerie/bern//2002
111////flyer//oh/mein/papa//stadtgalerie/bern//2002

206////blindekuh//mühlebachstrasse/148/8008/zürich/zh
207////blindekuh//mühlebachstrasse/148/8008/zürich/zh

places/to/be////
////genossenschaft/chornlade//fierzgasse/16/8005/zürich/zh
////filmpodium-kino/der/stadt/zürich/studio/4//nüschelerstrasse/11/8001/zürich/zh
////jazz/schule//süesswinkel/8/6004/luzern/lu
////bar/restaurant//jazzkantine/zum/graben//grabenstrasse/8/6004/luzern/lu
////kunstraum/walcheturm//kanonengasse/20/8004/zürich/zh

pathfinder/a/way/through/swiss/graphix

isbn////1-85669-367-8

pathfinder_book@hotmail.com

concept////happypets/products////sk/lam
design////happypets/products
editor////happypets/products

co-published/in/2003/by/idnpro/and/laurence/king/publishing/ltd

systems/design/limited
the/publisher/of/idnpro/publication
shop/c//s-9/gresson/street
wan/chai//hong/kong
tel////852/2528/5744
fax////852/2529/1296
email////info@idnworld.com
www.idnworld.com

laurence/king/publishing/ltd
71/great/russell/street
london/wc1b/3bp
united/kingdom
tel////44/20/7430/8850
fax////44/20/7430/8880
email////enquiries@laurenceking.co.uk
www.laurenceking.co.uk

many/thanks/to////
//// //diy////a---b////and-or////aubry/bastien////born/julia////cottenceau/geoffrey////gaillardot/julien/
////electronic/curry/ltd////schönwehrs////fehr/hansjakob////fulguro.////gtu////güdel/benjamin////kappeler/
marc////brunner/bianca////moiré////greber/andreas////la3l////lehmann/aude////mentary.com////norm////paulu
lauris////pussy/galhore////raar////judo////sonderegger/alex////woodtli/martin////s/k/lam////écal/école/
cantonale/d'art/de/lausanne////gilgen/marc////heruy/étienne////golgot////septembre